947.6 B83r
Bruchis, Michael.
  The Republic of Moldavia

THE REPUBLIC OF MOLDAVIA

FROM THE COLLAPSE OF THE SOVIET EMPIRE TO THE RESTORATION OF THE RUSSIAN EMPIRE

MICHAEL BRUCHIS

THE REPUBLIC OF MOLDAVIA

FROM THE COLLAPSE OF THE SOVIET EMPIRE TO THE RESTORATION OF THE RUSSIAN EMPIRE

Translated by Laura Treptow

EAST EUROPEAN MONOGRAPHS, BOULDER
Distributed by Columbia University Press
New York, 1996

EAST EUROPEAN MONOGRAPHS, NO. CDLXXVI

Copyright © 1997 by Michael Bruchis
ISBN 0-88033-373-1
Library of Congress Catalog Card Number 97-60359

Printed in the United States of America

CONTENTS

Introduction: The Romanians (Moldavians) East of
the Prut: Past and Present 7

Part I
Gorbachev's Reorganization and Soviet Moldavia

I. Attempts to Perpetuate Old-Fashioned Slogans 71

II. The Problem of Bessarabia and Transnistria 96

III. Debates in the Supreme Soviet
on the Molotov-Ribbentrop Pact 115

IV. Gorbachev as a Promoter of Soviet Imperialism 139

Part II
From the Collapse of the Soviet Empire (USSR)
to the Reorganization of the Russian Empire (CIS)

I. Between a Rock and a Hard Place 157

II. Manna for the *Mankurts* 189

Conclusion 199

INTRODUCTION

The Romanians (Moldavians) East of the Prut: Past and Present

Moldavians (*Moldoveni*) is the name given to the Romanians who live in the Eastern Carpathian region. In the USSR their language was the only representative of the Romance group of languages. According to the 1989 census, in Soviet Moldavia there were 2,794,700 (64.5%) Moldavians, 600,400 (13.8%) Ukrainians, 562,100 (13%) Russians, 153,500 (3.5%) Gagauz, 88,400 (2%) Bulgarians, 65,800 (1.5%) Jews and others. The Republic of Moldavia occupies a territory of 21,124 square miles. In 1940, when the *Union* republic was formed, the Moldavians constituted 70% of its population. The main cities of the republic and the number of their inhabitants in 1989 were: Chişinău (Kishinev), 720,000; Tiraspol, 182,000; Bălţi, 159,000; Bender (Tighina), 130,000. The republic has a high population density – 127 inhabitants per square kilometer.

1. Background.

The forefathers of the Moldavians[1] on both the eastern and the western side of the Prut river, as of the Romanian people as a whole, were the Dacians or the Getae (the Geto-Dacians). In the first century BC they were united by the king Burebista in a single state. In AD

---

[1] *Enciclopedia Sovietică Moldovenească* (ESM), 1975, vol. 5, p. 498.

106 the Dacians's state was crushed by force of arms, and part of its territory became a province of the Roman Empire.

In time the Dacians used their own language less and less, and their descendants began to feel increasingly part of the Roman world, becoming one with the descendants of the colonists brought in by the Roman conquerors.

Roman rule over Dacia (106-275) played an essential role in the ethnogenesis of the Romanian people both in the Roman province and in the other Dacian lands around it. The Romanization of the Dacians proceeded at an intense pace. In the course of some generations, a Dacian-Roman synthesis took place. By the middle of the third century all the inhabitants of Dacia spoke Vulgar Latin. At that time, under strong pressure of unceasing assaults by migratory peoples, the Emperor Aurelian decided to withdraw his legions and administration from Dacia. The majority of the descendants of the Romanized native Dacians and of the ex-servicemen remained on the left bank of the Danube, that is on the territory of Dacia, and had to face the domination of the migratory populations – the Goths and the Huns (275-566). From the sixth century, the Slavs settled in this area, who cohabited with the locals and were absorbed by them. Between the tenth and the thirteenth centuries, waves of Pecheneg, Cuman, and Tartar migrations occurred. When the almost thousand-year migratory movements ended, the descendants of the Daco-Romans, who at first withdrew to places of safety, especially to the Carpathians and to the forests,[2] began to move toward the lower areas once inhabited by their forefathers.

The emergence (after the end of the migratory movements) of the first administrative-political formations of the people inhabiting the Carpathian-Danubian region began long before the setting up of the Voievodate of Transylvania (the second half of the twelfth century), of the Wallachian state (the beginning of the fourteenth century), and of the Moldavian state (the middle of the fourteenth century). The foundation of the latter took place under voievod Bogdan on the territories east of the Carpathians.

---

[2] *Statul Naţional Unitar Român*, Bucureşti, 1975, p. 35.

INTRODUCTION

The development of Transylvania as an independent state was interrupted by the Hungarian conquest (from the eleventh until the thirteenth century). Wallachia's and Moldavia's rulers also had to face the danger threatening from invaders (from the Hungarians, the Tartars, the Poles, the Turks), but they succeeded to safeguard or regain independence during the fourteenth and fifteenth centuries. But even such outstanding voievods as Mircea the Old of Wallachia and Stephen the Great of Moldavia, despite their courageous resistance to the unceasing campaigns of the numerically superior hostile armies, were ultimately obliged to accept Turkish suzerainty and to pay tribute to the Ottoman Empire. Over the course of time the tribute exacted by the Turks from the subjected lands increased, becoming a heavy burden to the masses and leading to their pauperization. Thus, in the sixteenth century the tribute rose from 5,000 to 65,000 *ducats* in Moldavia.

Things were going from bad to worse not only in Moldavia but also in Wallachia and Transylvania as they were all caught in the centuries-old struggle in Southeastern Europe between the powerful states of those times. Side by side with the efforts of the Moldavians to put up resistance to the growing foreign oppression, their ethnic consciousness grew as they had close contacts with their brethren in Wallachia and Transylvania. Throughout the centuries this consciousness of ethnic community increased, despite the inner antagonisms and even the rivalry between certain Moldavian and Wallachian rulers which sometimes led to fratricidal wars — as, for example, between the Moldavian voievod Vasile Lupu and the Wallachian voievod Matei Basarab in the first half of the seventeenth century.

The short-lived political union of Wallachia, Transylvania, and Moldavia by the voievod Michael the Brave between 1599-1600 was not so much of immediate significance as of great importance in the long run. In all these provinces the mentioned union became a symbol of a national ideal for the next generation of native inhabitants, and firstly for their cultural development.

Not only after, but also before the momentary union under Michael the Brave there was evidence of a common Romanian ethnic self-consciousness of the Moldavians, Wallachians, and Transylvanians. Thus, Deacon Coresi from Târgoviște (Wallachia), who between 1559 and 1581 printed several religious books in Brașov (in Transylvania), asserted in the "epilogue" of his *Psalter* (1570) that the Romanians should have the sacred writings in their own language. The same wish was expressed in the *New Testament* printed in 1648 in Bălgrad (Alba Iulia) by the Transylvanian Metropolitan Simion Ștefan, as well as by the Metropolitan of Moldavia, Varlaam, whose main work, *Carte Românească de învățătură... (Romanian Preaching Book...)*, was printed in Iași (1643) and begins with "a foreword to all the Romanian people" ("*cuvânt împreună către toată semenția românească*").[3]

During the seventeenth and the eighteenth centuries the ethnic unity of the Moldavians, Wallachians, and Transylvanians, as well as their language community were demonstrated and propagated by such prominent figures as Grigore Ureche, Dimitrie Cantemir, Constantin Cantacuzino, Petru Maior, Gheorghe Șincai, and many others.

At the end of the eighteenth and the beginning of the nineteenth centuries, as a result of the process of disintegration of the Ottoman Empire, the territory of the Moldavian state, namely the region lying between the Eastern Carpathians and the Dniester river, was dismembered. Under the treaty of Kutchuk Kainardji (1774-1775) the Turks ceded the northwestern part of their vassal principality of Moldavia (Bucovina) to the Austrians. Later on, in 1812, under the Treaty of Bucharest, the Turks ceded the Moldavian territory between the Prut and the Dniester (Bessarabia) to the Russians. By that time the Moldavians from Bucovina and Bessarabia, or at least their majority, not only men of culture and science, were aware that the parts wrested from the Moldavian principality belonged to the Romanian people.

The subsequent development of Bucovina under the Habsburg Empire and that of Bessarabia under Romanov domination was quite different. In 1914 Lenin wrote that "oppressed nationalities inhabiting the (Russian) border regions have compatriots across the border who enjoy greater national independence (the Finns, the Swedes, the Poles, the Ukrainians, and the Romanians)." Concerning the

---

[3] Al. Rosetti et al. (eds.), *Istoria Literaturii Române*, vol. I, București, 1964, p. 338.

oppressed native inhabitants of Bessarabia, Lenin's statement referred to their compatriots's "greater national independence" not only in Moldavia west of the Prut (as an integral part of the Romanian state), but also in Bucovina (under Austrian domination). He asserted in another article that Russia's state system was "more backward and reactionary than that of any of the contiguous countries, beginning — in the West — with Austria."

During the centuries of Turkish domination the Moldavians had repeatedly asked for Russian aid and sometimes received it. They always supposed that their territorial integrity would be guaranteed while the Russian rulers nursed very far-reaching aims in Southeastern Europe which only partially were accomplished by the annexation of the territory lying between the Prut and the Dniester Rivers in 1812.

Until the beginning of the nineteenth century the term Bessarabia designated only the southern part of this territory, but for political purposes, mainly to "prove" that Bessarabia was a territory apart from the Moldavian Principality, Russian diplomacy extended the term to cover all of the area between the Prut and the Dniester.

In 1812, striving to set an attractive example to the Balkan Christians, Russia allowed the population of Bessarabia to preserve its own customs and laws. But the annexation by Russia caused the exodus of tens of thousands of Moldavian families to Moldavia west of the Prut. Moreover, the southern part of Bessarabia was spoiled during the 1806-1812 war. Nevertheless, owing to the intention of transforming Bessarabia into an example of treatment of peoples liberated from Ottoman vassalage, the new acquisition was not subjected in the first stage to the same oppressive rules as other provinces of the Russian Empire. Such preferential treatment contributed to the economic development of Bessarabia which before its annexation by Russia had been the most beautiful part of the Moldavian Principality.

However, the Russians changed their policy very soon. Thus, in 1913 a former Russian Minister of Education wrote that by the end of the 1820s the economic situation of the province was better under the administration of the Moldavian Principality than under the fifteen years of Russian domination.[4] Along with the change for the worse in the economy there occurred a steady process of cultural deterioration. The language of the native inhabitants was removed not only from the administration and schools, but, in time, even from church services. By the beginning of the twentieth century, as a result of the policy of Russification promoted by the authorities, neither Moldavian books, periodicals, or newspapers were published in Bessarabia.

Nevertheless, throughout the nineteenth century the Moldavians never lost their linguistic and national-ethnic identity. As in the previous centuries, men of culture endeavored to write in a language accessible to all three core provinces of the Romanian people. Thus, Ştefan Margela entitled his dual-language grammar book (1827) *Gramatică rusească şi rumânească* (*Russian and Romanian Grammar Book*); there were also two Romanian books published between 1862 and 1865 by Ion Doncev.

All the classic writers and the political figures of the nineteenth century — natives of Moldavia west of the Prut or Bucovina (Vasile Alecsandri, 1821-1890; Gheorghe Asachi, 1788-1869; Ion Creangă, 1837-1889; Mihai Eminescu, 1850-1889; Costache Negruzzi, 1808-1866; Bogdan Petriceicu Hasdeu, 1836-1907; Mihail Kogălniceanu, 1817-1891; Alecu Russo, 1819-1859) considered themselves Romanians and their language Romanian, and their historical homeland ancient Dacia.

Thus, for example, in such works as Alecsandri's *Emanciparea ţiganilor* (1844), *Deşteptarea României* (1848), *Hora Unirii* (1857), not only the "Romanian soul," the "people of Romania," the "Romanian heart" are praised, but also the extent of age-old lands of the Romanian people are described — "Beyond the Molna River, beyond the Milcov River, beyond the Prut River, beyond the Carpathians, areas which would include Bessarabia (beyond the Prut). Alecu Russo, a Bessarabian Moldavian, wrote that "Romanian is spoken everywhere in Moldavia, Wallachia, Bucovina, Transylvania, and the Banat." Meanwhile, the editor and director of *Dacia Literară*,

---

[4]Kass L., "Rossia da Dunae. Obrazovanie Bessarabskoi oblasti." *Bol'shaia Sovetskaia Entsiklopedia*. 1927, Moscow, vol. 6, p. 18.

Mihail Kogălniceanu, stressed that the magazine would be "a collection of Romanian literature, in which people from Moldavia, Transylvania, the Banat, and Bucovina would see their reflection as in a mirror," and that the editorial staff made an effort to see that "the Romanians would have a language and literature common to all of them."

The Unification of the core territories of the Romanian people was, for many of the above-mentioned figures, as well as for the Wallachians Nicolae Bălcescu (1819-1852), Cezar Bolliac (1813-1881), Dimitrie Bolintineanu (1819-1872), Ion Heliade Rădulescu (1802-1872), and the Transylvanians Simion Bărnuțiu (1808-1864), Timotei Cipariu (1805-1887), A. Mureşanu (1816-1863), and others, the most lofty ideal. Animated by love for their homeland, they were leaders of the 1848 revolution and later (in 1859) participants in the unification of the Danube Principalities (Wallachia and Moldavia west of the Prut).

In the 1880s, the idea of political unity of the Romanian people (including the Bessarabian Moldavians) and its territorial identity is reflected with geographical exactness and national firmness in the following lines of Eminescu's *Doina* (1883): "From Tisa to Dniester's tide/ All Romanians to me cried" (*"De la Nistru pân' la Tissa/ Tot Românu' plânsu-mi-s-a."*)

In 1859, after the union of Moldavia and Wallachia into one state, the process of Russification in Bessarabia was strengthened. By the beginning of the 1870s even clerical publications in the language of the native population were suppressed. Moreover, from the very beginning the Tsarist authorities pursued a policy of altering the demographic situation in the newly-conquered territory. Along with the immigration from the inner *gubernii* (provinces) of the Russian Empire, the immigration of Gagauz, Bulgarians, Germans, Jews, and people of other nationalities from foreign countries into Bessarabia was encouraged. According to the 1897 census the Moldavians constituted only 48 percent of the entire population of the province.[5] In addition, the figures of the same census gave evidence of almost the lowest level of literacy among the Moldavians (10.5% of men and

---

[5]*Bol'shaia Sovetskaia Entsiklopedia*, 1927, Moscow, vol. 6, p. 18.

1.7% of women) in comparison with the other nationalities of the province.[6]

The Russian revolution of 1905 and the great outburst of indignation in the country forced Tsar Nicholas II to repeal some legislation against ethnic minorities. Thus, for example, newspapers and magazines were once again permitted to appear in the languages of the non-Russian nationalities of the Empire. Under the circumstances, a group of patriotic-minded intellectuals founded a Moldavian newspaper called *Basarabia* in May 1906. The editor of *Basarabia*, E. Gavriliță, as well as his most active collaborator, P. Hallipa, strived to arouse the national-ethnical self-consciousness of the Moldavians. They nurtured patriotic plans and believed in the need for education and propaganda among the masses in the spirit of the essential demands of the time: "Justice, Freedom, and Land."

The great significance of the endeavors of *Basarabia* and of its successor, *Cuvânt Moldovenesc*, which was founded in 1913, lies in the fact that along with local authors (T. Roman, V. Oatu, A. Mateevici, S. Cujbă, I. Buzdugan, and others), they drew contributors from all the core provinces of the Romanian people.

2. Self-Determination and "the Question of Bessarabia" (1917-1940)

Soviet historians consider the October revolution in terms of the decisive events that took place in Bessarabia from the end of 1917 to the beginning of 1918 when, according to their theories, Soviet power was established in the province. In fact, after the seizure of power by the Bolsheviks in the center of Russia, the proclaimed right of nations to self-determination led in Bessarabia not to the establishment of Soviet power in the province, but to its freely uniting with Romania on 27 March (9 April) 1918.

Developments in Bessarabia turned out to be an accomplishment of the aims of its indigenous population. As early as the spring of 1917, as an effect of the Russian revolution of February 1917, the

---

[6]Pervaia vsesoiuznaia perepis' naselenia Rossiskoi imperii, 1897 g., Bessarabskaia gubernia, 1905, S. Petersburg, vol. 20.

revolutionary movement spread inside Bessarabia. Patriotic-minded Moldavians, both within the province and beyond (in Ukraine), started a struggle for the autonomy of Bessarabia. All the national organizations of the province supported the idea of the Council of representatives of Moldavian soldiers and officers on the Romanian front to convene a national assembly in Chişinău with a view to obtaining the autonomy of Bessarabia. As a result, the *National Assembly* (*Sfatul Ţării*) was founded in Bessarabia, which was made up of deputies representing various societies, associations, cooperatives, and, first of all, the Congress of the Moldavian Soldiers in Russia, the Gubernial Council of Peasants, and the Moldavian Party. On 2 (15) December 1917 *Sfatul Ţării* proclaimed that "from now on Bessarabia declares itself the Moldavian Democratic Republic, which will enter the make-up of the Russian Democratic Federative Republic as a participant with equal rights."[7]

Subsequent developments and chiefly the threat of military action on the part of the Russian army led to the breakdown of the relationship of dependence on Russia and to the unification of the Democratic Republic of Moldavia with Romania. The leaders of the movement for uniting Bessarabia with Romania were I. Inculeţ, P. Halippa, P. Erhan, I. Păscăluţă, I. Buzdugan, and I. Pelivan. Patriots from the historical Romanian provinces enthusiastically sided with the native population; the most important of these was the Transylvanian Onisifor Ghibu who published the newspaper *România Nouă* in Bessarabia.

In their overwhelming majority, those who fought for the breaking away of Bessarabia from Russia were people from the innermost Russian territories, who due to the war found themselves serving in the Russian Army of the Romanian front: I. Meleshin, I. Gudunov, I. Garkavy, I. Rozhkov, A. Vokov, and many others. Whereas not only the leaders, but also the supporters of *Sfatul Ţării* were mainly Romanians, the leaders and the deputies of the Soviet of Chişinău and of the Bessarabian region were in their overwhelming majority non-Bessarabians, and in the greatest part Russians.

---

[7]*Cuvânt românesc*, December 6, 1917.

Since the very beginning of the Romanian regime in Bessarabia, the Communist underground was led there by systematically infiltrated Soviet Communists, whose chief purpose was to prepare for the severance of the Romanian province from Romania. Proof of this consisted not only in systematically despatched subversive literature and money to instigate anti-Romanian actions, but also the despatch of communist underground organizers. The threat of losing Bessarabia again caused serious worry for all the Romanian governments that succeeded each other during the years 1918-1940. It was precisely those apprehensions that explained the economic policy of Romania's ruling circles with regard to Bessarabia. That policy had the worst possible effect on the latter's economic development and led to a standstill in its industry and a stagnation of its agriculture. While in 1919 the capital investment in Bessarabian industry was 6,2% of the overall capital investment in Romanian industry, by 1926 it was 2.65%, and in 1927 only 1.82%.[8] The condition of Bessarabian agriculture was no better. There was a considerable decrease in cereal crops and in cattle.[9] All that led to the pauperization of both the urban and rural population, to increased social contradictions, and therefore to increased danger to the authorities, resulting from underground activities of communist organizations in Bessarabia. The Romanian authorities, therefore, had good reasons for the special treatment of the communist movement not only in Bessarabia, which bordered on the Soviet Union, but all over their country. The communist underground movement, however, was not always a real power in Bessarabia. There were also mass anti-Romanian actions in the province, such as the Khotin uprising of 1919, organized and led by elements inimical to both Romania and Soviet Russia.

The very small number of Moldavians in the communist underground of Bessarabia throughout the period of 1918-1940 was chiefly due to its pronounced anti-Romanian character. When Bessarabia was included in the Romanian Kingdom at the beginning of 1918, the Moldavians (after having existed for over a century in

---

[8]*Anuarul Statistic al României*, 1922, Bucharest.

[9]Ibid., 1926; 1927; 1928.

the land of their ancestors as an oppressed nationality of the western border region of the Russian Empire) became an integral part of the predominant nation in Romania. Besides that, the very small number of Moldavians in the ranks of the Bessarabian workers (since most of the Moldavians of Bessarabia were peasants) made the demands of the communist underground for severance of the region from Romania incompatible with their national consciousness.

All that does not mean that during the entire 1918-1940 period there were not any anti-government riots and demonstrations in Bessarabia, in which the majority of participants were Moldavians. The latter, like the natives in other parts of Romania, were frequently rising against the authorities. However, such actions on the part of the Bessarabians did not, as a rule, have a mass character. They were all, without exception, demonstrations of peasants who did not aim to incorporate their territory into Soviet Russia, but who were simply demanding better living conditions within the framework of the Romanian state.

During the years 1918-1921, Moscow was tirelessly despatching its people across the river, from the left bank of the Dniester to Bessarabia for carrying out subversive activities, and supplied them with anti-Romanian literature and necessary means to start an armed struggle against the authorities at an opportue moment. At the same time, as direct dangers were threatening the Bolshevik regime from the outside as well as from domestic enemies, Moscow continued its efforts (particularly in 1920-1922) to ensure the security of its border with Romania along the Dniester river. Thus, for instance, in a note of 5 January 1921, Moscow suggested that Romania should limit the program of the assumed future Soviet-Romanian conference "only to solving the most urgent practical problems," which concerned the resumption of trade relations and the regulation of navigation on the Dniester.[10] Exactly a month later, in a note dated 15 February 1921, Moscow complained that the Romanian administration "not only does not act against rebellions which take place in Bessarabia, but even gives them its support," that such rebellions call for "constant vigilance" on the part of the Soviet authorities because "their purpose

---

[10]*Documenty vneshnei politiki S.S.S.R.*, 1959, Moscow, vol. 3, p. 475.

is not of a local, but of an overall character, and is part of an overall plan of struggle against the Soviet Republics."[11]

Early in 1921, after the Polish front ceased to exist, and following the victory of Moscow over Wrangel, the Soviet attitude toward the question of Bessarabia was not yet particularly hard. Even after the Russian-Romanian conference that took place in Warsaw at Russia's initiative in September 1921, and ended in failure because of Moscow's refusal to recognize the legitimacy of Bessarabia's incorporation in the Romanian state, even then the possibility of reaching a solution to the Bessarabian question that would have been acceptable to both sides was not possible. With Russia's position strengthened due to the end of the civil war, Moscow's attitude toward the Bessarabian question hardened as time went on. Nevertheless, on 20 November 1923 the Soviets signed an agreement with Romania called "Statute on Ways and Means for Prevention and Solution of Conflicts that May Arise on the Dniester River."[12] The signing of that agreement stipulated the resolution of border incidents by a joint Soviet-Romanian commission.[13] All this demonstrated that together with the hardening at that time of Moscow's position on the Bessarabian question, the Soviet Union was interested in establishing a strict border regime along the Dniester river that would prevent any kind of infringement on the part of Romania, that it renounced the use of the river not only for despatching agents to Bessarabia, but also for sending across subversive literature and other means of anti-Romanian activity. That, however, did not mean that Moscow had altogether renounced the leadership and control of the communist movement in Romania and Bessarabia. In Soviet historical works one repeatedly finds it mentioned how, after the above-mentioned agreement had been signed on 20 November 1923, Bessarabian and Romanian Communists were leaving the country to avoid repressions and were going to Russia to receive instructions and then return to

---

[11]Ibid., p. 520.

[12]Ibid., 1962, Moscow, vol. 6, pp. 512-16.

[13]Ibid., p. 512.

Romania, although not by crossing the Dniester but in a roundabout way via Germany or Austria.[14]

Moscow made considerable efforts for a new Soviet-Romanian conference with the purpose of "resolving all the controversial problems."[15] Such a conference took place in Vienna between 27 March and 2 April 1924, yet Moscow's claim of having a plebiscite in Bessarabia did not succeed, and the conference ended in a fiasco.

Unable to take military action against Romania, Moscow developed a vast plan of activities that were intended to remind the whole world of the existence of a serious territorial problem in Southeastern Europe[16] and of Russia's historical right to demand the return of Bessarabia to the Ukraine.

Part of the above-mentioned plan was created by the Bessarabia Association (Obshchestvo Bessarabtsev) in Moscow, in May 1924. The Bessarabian Association, whose statute was recognized in November 1924 by the Sovnarkom of the USSR,[17] was in close contact not only with similar associations in the big cities of Russia and the Ukraine, but also with the Bessarabian societies for friendship with USSR that existed in many European countries — France, Germany, Austria, Czechoslovakia, and others.

From the ranks of former Bessarabian communist underground activists, who left Bessarabia at different times, Moscow recruited the leadership of the Moldavian Autonomous Republic on the left bank of the Dniester River after the unsuccessful conference that took place in Vienna in 1924. The bureau of the Moldavian party regional committee, the government, and other organizations in authority of that artificially created administrative-political formation consisted in their overwhelming majority of former Bessarabian activists — I. Badeev, Kh. Bogopolsky, S. Bubnovsky, G. Buchushkan, K. Galitsky, I. Krivorukov, K. Rayevich, G. Stary, A. Stroev, K. Kolostenko, and many others. The idea of creating a Moldavian

---

[14]ESM, 1974, vol. 4, p. 91.

[15]*Izvestia*, December 9, 1923.

[16]*Documenty vneshnei politiki S.S.S.R.*, 1963, Moscow, vol. 7, pp. 181-182.

[17]ESM, 1970, vol. 1, p. 260.

Autonomous Republic was to serve as a permanent reminder of Moscow's firm stand on Bessarabia, for showing the world that it would not give up, under any circumstances, its intention of taking possession of Bessarabia at the first opportune moment. The following data are an eloquent testimony to the fact that the Moldavian Autonomous Republic was an artificially created administrative-political formation: for example, at the end of 1924 Moldavians represented only 6.3% of the members of Communist Party organizations in the republic, and only 4% in its affiliated organizations.[18]

Moscow was interested in having subversive forces acting not only within Romania, for the severance of Bessarabia from it, but also in Bessarabia itself to provoke serious popular unrest in the region. That was supposed to be the proof of the Bessarabians's desire to free themselves from Romanian rule at any price.

Already in 1918, when detachments of armed people were transferred across the Dniester from the Ukraine for anti-Romanian activities,[19] a Petrograd worker, the Russian Andrey Klyushinov, arrived in Bessarabia and began organizing a revolutionary committee. Toward the end of 1923 he became secretary of the South Bessarabian underground communist committee, and immediately after the unsuccessful Vienna conference, preparations for active anti-Romanian actions began.[20] As to the causes which accelerated the peasant uprising in southern Bessarabia in September 1924, they were (according to a Soviet Ukrainian historian) two: the activities of the communist underground, under the leadership of Klyushnikov, in connection with the failure of the Vienna conference and "the terrible famine caused by an unprecedented dry fall, snowless winter, and dry summer, which resulted in appalling poor wheat and maize crops."[21]

---

[18]Bochacher M., *Moldavia*, M.-L., 1926, pp. 42, 44.

[19]*Luptători ai mișcării revoluționare ilegale*, p. 89.

[20]ESM, 1973, vol. 3, p. 304; *Letopis vazhneishikh sobytii istorii kompartii Moldavii*, Kishinev, 1976, p. 209.

[21]Smishko, P. *Borot'ba trudiashchikh ukrainskikh pridunaiskikh zemel'za vozz'ednannia z U.R.S.R. 1917-1940*. L'viv, 1969, p. 164.

INTRODUCTION 21

The southern Bessarabian uprising (Tatarbunar, 1924), just as the northern Bessarabian one (Khotin, 1919), occurred in those areas in which there were very important demographic changes resulting from Tsarist Russia's imperialistic policy of settling in Bessarabia large numbers of people from the central Russian and Ukrainian regions, as well as from other countries. The Khotin uprising was, in fact, not only anti-Romanian, but also anti-Russian, while that of Tatarbunar (1924) was on the one hand anti-Romanian and on the other hand pro-Soviet. Those two anti-Romanian uprisings in Bessarabia over the 1918-1940 period were mainly Ukrainian in character because the overwhelming majority of their participants were not Moldavians, but Ukrainians.

3. Under Soviet Rule

Moscow's use of such events as the Tatarbunar and the Hotin uprisings as a proof of the uninterrupted twenty-two year struggle of the entire population of Bessarabia to join the USSR, "for unification with the MASSR (Autonomous Soviet Socialist Republic of Moldavia)"[22] was in fact a distortion of the real state of affairs. Moscow's thesis that the majority of Bessarabia's population demonstrated its wish to see Bessarabia returned to the USSR was widely circulated within the Soviet Union, and in all pro-Soviet associations, societies, groups, etc. outside the Soviet Union. In the spirit of that thesis an ultimatum was composed on 26 June 1940, which asserted that Bessarabia was chiefly populated by Ukrainians.[23]

In 1924, forming the Autonomous Moldavian Soviet Socialist Republic on the left, Ukrainian, bank of the Dniester, Moscow conducted its policy with the help of the Bessarabians who happened to be on Soviet territory after the unification of Bessarabia with Romania in 1918. After the Stalinist purges of 1937-1938, together with party-state activists of the Autonomous Republic, the leading cadres of culture and literature also ended up being repressed. The

---

[22]Cornovan, D. et al. (eds.), *Ocherk istorii kommunisticheskoi partii Moldavii*, 2nd ed., Chişinău, 1968, p. 193.

[23]"Pravda," June 29, 1940.

origin of these cadres was mostly from the right, Bessarabian, bank of the Dniester. Replacing the leaders of the Autonomous Republic chosen by Moscow were new people, mainly from among the activists of lower-ranking organizations in the Ukraine and the Autonomous Republic, as well as newly-promoted workers recruited to Party and State activity for the first time. Among those occupying the highest positions were people who were unfamiliar with the history and culture of the Moldavians and, frequently, with their language (P. Borodin, K. Konstantinov, F. Brovko, S. Zelenchuk, and others). Many were the Russianized and Ukrainianized descendants of those Moldavians who had left the Moldavian Principality during the Russian-Turkish wars of the eighteenth and nineteenth centuries and resettled in parts of the Ukraine remote from the principality (Kirovofrad, Nikolaev, and other provinces) or in areas along the left bank of the Dniester. Acting as compliant enforcers of Moscow's nationalities policy in the Autonomous Moldavian Soviet Socialist Republic, they helped to achieve significant successes in severing the Moldavians from the east bank of the Dniester from Romanian culture and transforming their language into a Moldavian-Russian-Ukrainian jargon.

After the Soviet Union took over Bessarabia, the officials of Moldavian and non-Moldavian extraction were transferred to Chişinău and placed in positions of authority in the *Union* Moldavian Soviet Socialist Republic formed by the Supreme Soviet of the USSR on 2 August 1940. The Moldavian Soviet Socialist Republic was created when Romania was forced to cede Bessarabia, the northern part of Bucovina, and the Northwestern part of Dorohoi county of Moldavia west of the Prut to the Soviet Union. The central counties of Bessarabia were included by Moscow within the newly created *Union* republic along with a part (less than a half) of the Autonomous Moldavian Soviet Socialist Republic. The northern part of Bucovina, together with the Bessarabian counties of Akkerman, Ismail, Hotin, and part of Dorohoi county were added to the Ukraine, along with the major part of the Autonomous Moldavian Soviet Socialist Republic which was thus liquidated at this time. The dismemberment of Bessarabia and the actual liquidation of the autonomous republic were very much at variance with the line of Soviet propaganda during the preceding sixteen years (1924-1940), when the current slogan was

INTRODUCTION

the unification of Bessarabia with the Autonomous Moldavian Soviet Socialist Republic.

Moscow's policy aimed at severing the ties of the Moldavians east of the Prut with Romanian history and culture. Historians, linguists, literary scholars, and critics were encouraged to produce publications which would not only justify the annexation of Bessarabia by the Tsarist Empire in 1812 and by the Soviet Union in 1940, but which would also bolster a theory that the Moldavians east of the Prut became a separate nation with their own language as early as the past century.

The attempts to realize such a policy were interrupted by the war, but resumed immediately after it ended. In the first post-war year the communist organization of the republic grew by more than two and a half times — from 5649 to 15,853 members and candidate members of the Communist Party.[24] But, as in the pre-war year, from the First Secretary of the Central Committee of the Moldavian Communist Party to the functionaries at the lowest levels of the hierarchy in the district committees, all were new-comers from the left bank of the Dniester, as well as demobilized communists from the Soviet army and people who had come from other Soviet republics.[25] Most of these people did not know the language of the Moldavians, and were obliged, in order to communicate with them, "to turn to interpreters."[26]

In the conditions of the late 1940s, when Moscow decided that the time had come to implement the total collectivization of agriculture in the Bessarabian sector of Soviet Moldavia as well, together with the means of coercion and outright force, it considered it necessary to apply another method of persuasion, as the lack of a "link with the masses" became a serious obstacle on the path to achieving its goal. This explains why 1287 (53.87%) of the 2389

---

[24]Binilishvili et al (eds.), *Rost i organizatsionnoe ukreplenie kommunisticheskoi partii Moldavii*. 1924-1974, Chişinău, 1976, p. 169.

[25]Shemiakov, D., "Letopis' partiinogo stroitel'stva." *Kommunist Moldavii*, nr. 6, p. 90.

[26]Lutokhin, I., "Letopis' partiinogo stroitel'stva," in *Kommunist vspominaiut*," Chişinău, 1974, p. 23.

persons selected in 1949 as candidate members of the Communist Party were Moldavians.[27] Having opened the door to the Communist Party to Bessarabians (in the first instance from among those who had fought in the war against Germany, and later distinguished industrial workers, kolkhozniks, and graduates of Soviet educational institutions), the Kremlin rulers created a basis of support for themselves among people who prepared to sacrifice the national interests of their own people for class interests, which in the interpretation of Soviet ideologists were identical with Moscow's aims.

In the first post-war years the left bank officials of Moldavian extraction who were placed in positions of authority in the Union Soviet Socialist Republic of Moldavia tried to impose their Moldavian-Russian-Ukrainian jargon upon the Bessarabian Moldavians as the national language of the republic (this was the language in which textbooks, newspapers, works of fiction, etc. were printed on the left bank of the Dniester). From the very beginning, however, they encountered opposition from Bessarabian cultural figures, in particular from writers, linguists, and literary critics who, in the interwar period, had written in unadulterated Romanian, and in the new created conditions undertook efforts to save their language from being transformed into a Russified jargon. They succeeded due to two factors. Firstly, the best known of the Bessarabian writers (E. Bukov, B. Istru, A. Lupan, G. Meniuc, etc.) supported the annexation of Bessarabia by the Soviet Union in 1940. Secondly, because of their broadcasting on Soviet radio and writing in the Soviet press during the World War II, these writers were looked upon by Moscow as having made a contribution to the defeat of Germany. In view of their demonstrated loyalty to the Soviet cause, Moscow did not consider it appropriate to support the attacks of the "left-bankers" in Soviet Moldavia against them for their devotion to the Romanian language.

Moscow's attitude in this case was "a step back" from the point of view of the Soviet Communist Party's language policy. It led to

---

[27]Grecul, A., *Moldavskaia sovetskaia gosudarstvennost' i bessarabskii vopros*, Chişinău, 1974, p. 119.

the identification of the literary form of Moldavian with the Romanian language. It was, in the full sense of the word, a great victory of the Bessarabians (E. Bucov, G. Bogaci, V. Coroban, and many others) over the new-comers from the left bank of the Dniester (N. Coval, D. Tcaci, P. Tereshchenko, I. Ceban, I. Varticean, and others). However, in the long run, it proved to be a Pyrrhic victory, because Moscow's "step back" was followed by "two steps forward," in the sense that concomitant with the "step back" were two incessant processes. On the one hand, a continuous reduction of the most important social functions of the Moldavians's national language, and, on the other hand, a systematic transformation of the latter's *conversational form* into a Moldavian-Russian jargon.

Side by side with a gradual supplanting in such a way of the Moldavian language by the Russian language, a systematic rewriting of the Moldavians's national history took place. Due to S. Afteniuc, N. Bereznyakov, S. Tsaranov, D. Shemyakov, A. Esaulenko, A. Lazarev, and other left-bank scholars who held key positions in the republic's historical sciences, theses and postulates were developed that were to form the basis of a theory of Soviet statehood of the Moldavian people and the formation of the Moldavian Socialist nation. As a result of their endeavors, analogical theses such as the following were created:

"The Moldavians who lived in Bessarabia and on the left-bank Moldavia did not and could not participate in the process of the formation of the Romanian nation, just as the Romanians did not and could not participate in the process of formation of the Moldavian nation, ...the Eastern Moldavians continued to develop separately, forming the independent Moldavian nation, endowed with an independent culture and separate language."[28]

Under the completely Russianized Ivan Bodiul who, for almost twenty years (1961-1980), was First Secretary of the Moldavian Communist Party, the process of denationalization of the native population of the republic and of the actual transformation of the latter into an ordinary *oblast* was enormously accelerated. Bodiul was

---

[28]Lazarev, A., *Moldavskaia sovetskaia gosudartsvennost'i bessarabskii vopros*, Chișinău, 1974, pp. 116, 749.

making efforts to create a base of support for himself in the form of obedient cadres not only from among the left-bankers, but also the Bessarabian Moldavians, and to train these cadres in a spirit of identification of what they called class interests with Moscow's interests. In February 1967 he stated: "The children and future generations must fully understand that their fathers never conceived of a life separate from Russia."[29] In 1971 Bodiul pointed out that "the *all-union character* of the country's economic life had been strengthened," "the process of economic interaction between the republics, territories (*krayev*), *oblasts* had been rendered immeasurably more active, and that the interchange of cadres had been expanded."[30] That the *all-union character* had been strengthened not only in the economic, but also in other areas of life in the republic is confirmed, for example, by the fact that among the delegates with a decisive vote from the Moldavian party organization at the 24th Congress of the Communist Party of the Soviet Union, Bessarabians comprised an insignificant minority.[31] The *all-union character* was also strengthened by virtue of the fact that in the second half of the 1970s "more than a quarter of all the families were mixed"[32] in the republic. This *all-union character* of the republic finds expression in yet another circumstance. Alongside the increase in the multi-nationality of its population on the one hand, and in the number of mixed families on the other hand, a phenomenon such as the *multi-nationality of individuals* can also be observed. Each person who was sent to work in Soviet Moldavia, whether a high-ranking party functionary or a simple worker, automatically became a citizen of the republic and an integral part of the people of the Moldavian Soviet Socialist Republic. This explains how, for example, Petr

---

[29]Bodiul, I., "O podgotovke k 50-letiu velikoi oktiabrskoi revoliutsii i zadachakh partiinoi organizatsii respubliki." *Sovetskaia Moldavia*, February 16, 1971.

[30]*Sovetskaia Moldavia*, February 27, 1971.

[31]*Letopis' vazhneishikh sobytii istorii kommunisticheskoi partii Moldavii.* Kishinev, 1976, pp. 597-8.

[32]Entelis G., "Omogenitate," *Moldova Socialistă*, June 28, 1977.

INTRODUCTION 27

Zaistev, a worker who came to Soviet Moldavia in 1962, became, within a year, a deputy of the Supreme Soviet of the Republic.[33]

While demanding of the party organization of the republic that they "conduct an uncompromising struggle against all manifestations of nationalism, parochialism, the preaching of national exclusiveness, isolationism, etc.,"[34] the Central Committee under Bodiul began to appoint to traditional Moldavian positions persons of non-Moldavian extraction, new-comers from other republics. For example, following Y.S. Grosul's death, A.A. Zhuchenko was placed at the head of the Academy of Sciences of the Moldavian Soviet Socialist Republic in 1977. People of non-Moldavian as well as of Moldavian extraction (including Bessarabians), who had demonstrated their readiness to carry out blindly any and every bidding of the party organs, were selected to head ideological and scientific organizations and institutions.

The measures taken by the authorities and aimed ultimately at the denationalization of the indigenous population of Soviet Moldavia alarmed the patriotically inclined national intelligentsia and students. This alarm found its clearest expression in the 1970s in such works of literature as the play *Doina*[35] and the novelette *Perfume of Ripened Quince*.[36] Such works aroused the national consciousness of the Moldavians east of the Prut. This was especially the case as a number of Soviet scientists had openly raised the question of "the contemporary assimilation of the population in the USSR being a completely natural and normal process,"[37] "of ethnic merging of peoples and nations,"[38] which "will take place in the foreseeable future."[39]

---

[33]Grecul, A., op. cit., p. 194.

[34]Cornovan, D. et al. *Ocherki...*, p. 429.

[35]Druță, I., "Teatr," *Doina*, Moscow, 1971, no. 135-165.

[36]Druță, I., "Iunost," *Zapakh speloi aivy*, Moscow, 1973, no. 9, pp. 4-44.

[37]Pereverdentsev, V.

[38]Kislitsyn, I.

[39]Semionov, P.

THE REPUBLIC OF MOLDAVIA

After the April 1985 Plenum of the Central Committee of the Communist Party of the Soviet Union

In the twenty years that Bodiul was first secretary of the Central Committee, he faithfully tried to implement Moscow's nationalities policy and became the most odious figure in the eyes of the patriotic-minded national intelligentsia of the republic. At the same time, he set out to color favorably the economics of Soviet Moldavia. And his behavior in this respect led to lawless actions on a mass scale. In the end, Bodiul's failures in the fields both of nationalities policy and mainly in economics caused his removal from office as head of the republic in December 1980. Nominally, he was promoted to the higher position of deputy chairman of the Council of Ministers of the USSR, but in fact it was an honorable demotion for which he had to thank to Brezhnev.

After Brezhnev's death, Andropov launched an attack on his rival, N. Shchelokov, the minister of internal affairs of the USSR. The latter had been intimate with Brezhnev. They had worked together both in the Ukrainian Soviet Socialist Republic before World War II, and in Soviet Moldavia in the years 1951-1952. Shchelokov continued to work in Soviet Moldavia until his appointment as minister of internal affairs in 1966.[40] The sharp criticism to which Moscow subjected the Central Committee of the Moldavian Communist organization on 6 December 1983 was spearheaded first and foremost against Shchelokov and Bodiul. Andropov had time to square accounts only with Shchelokov. Chernenko, however, being at one time elected deputy of the Supreme Soviet of the USSR by one of the constituencies of the Moldavian Soviet Socialist Republic, was friendly with Bodiul and not at all in a hurry to punish him. But Gorbachev did it. Bodiul was first forced to retire and, after that, to leave the Supreme Soviet before the expiration of his term of office.[41]

In the whole Brezhnev period, Soviet officials, as well as obedient specialists in social sciences, invariably extolled the "revolutionary, Marxist-Leninist" view of socialism of the leadership.

---

[40] ESM, 1977, vol. 7, p. 414.

[41] *Sovetskaia Moldavia*, April 20, 1986.

On the other hand, violations of moral and ethical norms, the gaining of unearned income and other similar phenomena were always officially condemned in the USSR. The 1961 program of the Communist Party of the Soviet Union, for example, asserted that "the moral code of the builder of communism" should comprise such principles as "an uncompromising attitude to injustice, parasitism, dishonesty, careerism, and greed."[42] The seventy-year rule of the Communist Party of the Soviet Union proves that, at congresses, plenums, and conventions of the party, as well as of Soviet bodies, consideration will be always given also to the shortcomings and deficiencies of Soviet realities. But by now there were quite distinct indications of the continuous and growing cult of its current general secretary's personality. The developments in the USSR showed that the time was not far distant when members of the CPSU Politburo would extol General Secretary Gorbachev (if he had continued in power for some years to come) in the same way that they had praised Brezhnev. For example, as Eduard Shevarnadze said at the twenty-sixth Congress of the CPSU, in February 1981: "The report of Leonid Ilich Brezhnev... is not only an epoch-making document, but also a living organism all of whose cells are linked with each member of our society. It seems that this living organism has absorbed all the qualities of its author, of its creator, our wise leader, the great Leninist revolutionary Leonid Ilich Brezhnev."[43] Gorbachev repeatedly stated (and Soviet public figures reiterated) that openness (*glasnost'*) in the USSR should be broadened, and that Soviet society should not be content with half-truths as in the seventies and the beginning of the eighties.[44] Meanwhile, not only half-truths, but glaring untruths continued to be a hallmark of the Soviet realities. Soviet Moldavia can serve as a good example in this respect.

Thus, in June 1986, four months *before* a condemnatory resolution of October 1986 of the Central Committee of the Communist Party of the Soviet Union was adopted, First Secretary

---

[42]"Programma kommunisticheskoi partii Sovetskogo Soiuza," Moscow, 1973, p. 120.

[43]*Pravda*, February 26, 1986.

[44]Ibid.

of the Moldavian Communist organization S. Grossu made speeches at different forums in which he, as usual, spoke about some shortcomings, but at the same time emphasized that "The last ten months of the year (1986) show that positive changes have begun to occur in the thinking and actions of our people... The rate of increase of industrial production in five months... exceeded the rate attained last year by more than double. Fourteen percent more fixed capital was placed into operation in capital construction compared to the corresponding period of last year, and thirty-nine percent more housing was introduced. Meat production increased by eighteen percent, while milk production increased by five percent.[45] Meanwhile, *after the October 1986 resolution* was adopted, Grossu confessed at a plenum of the Central Committee of the Communist organization of the republic that in Moldavia "there is not a single branch in which cover-ups were not exposed," that "the proportion of units where... deceiving the state by exaggerated accounts has increased from 7.6% to 10.8% in the first half of the current year (1986) in comparison with the corresponding period of the last one," that "all cities and districts have been contaminated by exaggerated accounts," and that "similar grave transgressions took place in industry and agriculture, in transport and in construction, as well as in the sphere of public service."[46]

Not only Grossu and other participants in the mentioned plenum, but also the resolution of the latter disclosed that, right up to the last, with Moscow's control of the republic, falsifications, swindles, and so on were practiced on a large scale. This is why, as it was divulged in Grossu's report, only in the last two and a half years in Moldavia "ten thousand members were expelled from the Communist Party," and twenty seven deputies were removed from the Supreme Soviet of the republic."[47] The speakers at the Plenum of October 1986 used, for realities of Soviet Moldavia and the behavior of its officials, such terms as "falsifications," "frauds," "cover-ups," "subjectivism,"

---

[45] *Sovetskaia Moldavia*, June 8, 1986.

[46] Ibid., October 24, 1986.

[47] Ibid.

INTRODUCTION   31

"bribery," "hare-brained plans," "dread of superiors," "social demagogy," etc.[48]

For the first time, blame for the ingrained dishonesty in the life of the republic was laid publicly on the former first secretary I. Bodiul. So that the failure of his hare-brained plans could not be found out, Bodiul had created a republic headquarters, which consisted of seven members and alternate members of the Central Committee of the Moldavian Communist Party and seven members of the republic's Council of Ministers. That body, as the speakers at the plenum asserted, "became, in fact, a headquarters for organizing exaggerated accounts." A body of "falsification and constraint under duress," whose participants "turned into jugglers, who, out of nothing, could create any quantity in any agricultural production." In Bodiul's period, Eremei (who was at one time first vice-chairman of the republic's Council of Ministers) told the participants at the plenum that special routes "were worked out for visitors and inspectors. In order to display outward appearances of progress and prosperity, commonly owned cattle were driven from one collective farm to another."

In connection with the October 1986 plenum the following should be emphasized. Many members of the Central Committee, up to and including its Bureau, were also in Bodiul's period top-level party and government functionaries (S. Grossu, G. Eremei, I. Kalin, and others). Grossu mentioned his own "neglect of duty" and qualified his weaknesses as "flabbiness, inconsistency, and liberalism with respect to delinquencies of certain high-level executives." However, he resolutely criticized, for example, E. Kalenik: "I would like to remind him and all those who allude to circumstances, that the rules of the Communist Party of the Soviet Union demand from each of us to combat ostentation, conceit, complacency, to rebuff firmly all attempts at suppressing criticism, to resist all actions injurious to the party and the state, and to give information about them to party bodies up to and including the Central Committee of the Communist Party of the Soviet Union. And never was anybody forbidden the use of this right." According to the rules, every member of the

---

[48]Ibid., October 25, 1986.

Communist Party of the Soviet Union indeed had the duties and the right to which he referred. But Grossu himself did not fulfill these duties and did not use that right, either in Bodiul's period or in his own.

As a matter of fact, Grossu, as the secretary of the Central Committee charged with agriculture under Bodiul, was an accessory to the latter's hare-brained plans which led the republic to the brink of an ecological catastrophe. On the other hand, on 11 March 1983, i.e., some years after Bodiul's removal, Grossu, as first secretary of the Central Committee, made an appeal "to intensify intransigence towards any manifestations of national narrow-mindedness."[49] The same occurred at a December 1986 conference of Soviet Moldavian professors and lecturers specializing in social sciences, where S. Grossu assisted; it was stressed that "a certain proportion of students and pupils show political short-sightedness and national narrow-mindedness, and make immature declarations." In order to uproot such phenomena, the specialists in social sciences of Soviet Moldavia were asked to "instill a deep understanding in students and pupils of the Russian language's role as a means of strengthening the international unity of the Soviet people."[50]

Perhaps the most significant display of Grossu's disregard of the Moldavians's material and spiritual values was the "Thesis" adopted by the Central Committee of the Moldavian Communist Party, the Presidium of the Supreme Soviet, and the republic's Council of Ministers in November 1988. Section three in particular concerned the national question and the language policy. Statements of the "Thesis" that "Moldavian and Romanian are languages of the same Romance group," that Moldavian is an "equal in rights and independent (*de sine stătătoare*) language," that there is "a national tradition of using the Slavic (Cyrillic) writing," that "the Cyrillic alphabet corresponds as a whole with the phonetic nature of the Moldavian language," and so on, aroused the indignation not only of

---

[49] Ibid., March 12, 1983.

[50] See "Vysokoe prizvanie obskchetvove dov," *Sovetskaia Moldavia*, December 5, 1986.

the patriotic-minded national intellegentsia of Soviet Moldavia, but of the overwhelming majority of the republic's indigenous population.

Thus, from the very beginning the "Thesis" proved to be a fiasco. In a brief space of time the weekly magazine *Literatura şi Arta* (*Literature and Art*) received thousands of letters signed by more than two hundred thousand inhabitants of Soviet Moldavia and by people beyond its boundaries who disapproved of and even severely criticized the "Thesis."

In 1987, the well-known Moldavian novelist and play-wright Ion Druţă pointed out not only that the reckless land reclamation and excessive use of chemicals turned vast fertile fields of the republic into salt-marshes and led to the contamination of its natural resources, but also that the language policy promoted by the authorities transformed spoken Moldavian language into an incomprehensible jargon.[51] The writer condemned in this way not only Bodiul and his deeds, but, in fact, the behavior of the leadership headed by Grossu as well.

The trinity formula Land — History — Language, which was launched by Druţă, found a broad response among the indigenous population of Soviet Moldavia. The patriotic-minded men of science, culture, and literature came out in a united front for the national demands and aspirations of the Moldavians. Their struggle for national awareness amongst the native population found a fertile soil. The furtherance of the Communist leadership's aims met with strong opposition all over the territory of Soviet Moldavia.

The Moldavian Popular Front movement, the "Alexe Mateevici" Association, the republic's Writers' Union and its magazines *Nistru* and *Literatura şi Arta* (*Literature and Art*) were the most outspoken mouthpieces of the national trends of that time. During the years 1988 and 1989, tens of thousands of workers, peasants, school teachers, students, engineers, physicians, etc. from different towns and villages gathered many times in Chişinău to protest against: a) the "Thesis" of the Central Committee; b) the mass immigration from other republics to Moldavia, and the exodus of Moldavian youth to

---

[51]Druţă, I., "Zelenyi list, voda i znaki prepinania." *Literaturnaia Gazeta*, Moscow, July 29, 1987.

remote territories of the USSR organized by the authorities; c) the dismemberment of Bessarabia by Moscow in 1940, and so on. But first and foremost the participants in every such meeting spoke out not only for the need to broaden the social functions of the Moldavian language, by means of enforcing its status as the official language of the republic, but also for the transition from its Slavic alphabet to the Latin one as more adequate to a Romance language.

Grigore Vieru, Leonida Lari, Dumitru Matcovschi, Nicolae Dabija, Valentin Mândâcanu, Silviu Berejan, Ion Demeniuc, Nicolae Mătcaş, Constantin Tănase, Vasile Bahnaru, and many other men of literature, science, and culture came out in a united front for the salvation of the national values of the Moldavian people and had the overwhelming majority of the Moldavians against the efforts of the authorities to continue their policy of Russification.

As a counterbalance to the strengthening in ever larger strata of the indigenous population of national-patriotic tendencies, the "Unity" ("Edinstvo") movement sprang up in Soviet Moldavia, a movement which grouped representatives of the non-indigenous population of the republic and Russianized Moldavians as well as the nomenclature of Moldavian extraction. Among the spokesmen of this movement were A. Lisetsky, V. Yakovlev, A. Borş, V. Stati, and many others. Their overwhelming majority had been ardent supporters of the nationalities policy of the Communist Party of the Soviet Union in Brezhnev's period, but turned their coat and proclaimed themselves to be faithful followers of Gorbachev and his *Perestroika*.

The historian A. Lisetsky, for example, as early as 1977, rejected the view of those who feared that increasing population mobility and increasing exchange of cadres among the republics of the USSR "may lead to denationalization or Russification." Such fears of patriotically-inclined representatives of the non-Russian Soviet peoples and nationalities met with his decided rebuttal, as reflecting — in his words — "a yearning for national isolation and narrow-mindedness."[52] At the same time he formulated the thesis that "it is not necessary for the principle of strict proportionality, corresponding

---

[52]Lisetsky, A., *Vorposy natsional noi politiki K.P.S.S v usloviakh razvitogo sotsialisma. Po materialam Moldavskoi S.S.R.*, Chişinău, 1977, p. 58.

to the specific weight of the basic ethnic groups in the population, to be observed in any particular elective, administrative, public, or economic organ."[53] Thus, in Brezhnev's period Lisetsky took on the role of mouthpiece for those forces in Soviet Moldavia (mainly newcomers from outlying regions of the USSR or Russianized Moldavians from the left bank of the Dniester) who sought to crush the "faith in their just cause" of representatives of the indigenous population and to deprive them of any advantages that they could have from the fact that the republic bore their name.

In time, Lisetsky became one of the most aggressive members of "The Internationalist Movement to Guard the *Perestroika*" (as "Unity" was called by its members). *Literatura şi Arta* asserted in an editorial that on June 18, 1989 Lisetsky recoursed to an outright instigation, warning Gorbachev and the KGB, as well as the local authorities, that the Moldavians intended to make a pogrom of the Russian-speaking population of the republic on June 26-27.[54]

Another "internationalist" was the linguist A. Borş who did not know the national language of his people in its literary form and did not write in this language. In 1970, for example, he stated that "all the most important official documents are written and published in Moldavian and Russian,"[55] although he knew very well that official documents in Soviet Moldavia were altogether written in Russian. In the circumstances of the fearless struggle of the patriotic-minded national intelligentsia for replacing the Slavic alphabet of Moldavian with the Latin one, Borş attempted to undermine their efforts. In his article, *Slavic writing among the Eastern Romanic peoples* (August 1988), the eighty-year old former head of the Moldavian department at the University of Chişinău, in contradiction not only with the truth, but with common knowledge among the overwhelming majority of the republic's national intelligentsia, wrote a) that "the Moldavians have been using Slavic writing uninterruptedly until today," and b) that "the Cyrillic alphabet can reproduce with the highest possible

---

[53]Ibid., p.139.

[54]*Literatura şi Arta*, July 13, 1989.

[55]"ESM," 1970, vol. 1, p. 423.

precision all the richness of the Moldavian language and the peculiarity of its phonetic system."[56]

The fact that "all the newspapers of the republic printed Borş's article in its integral form" shows that he was playing into the hands of the republic's authorities.

The strong opposition to the replacing of the Slavic alphabet by the Latin one can be explained by the fact that the Russians and the Russianized people in Soviet Moldavia, who always felt that they belonged to the dominant nation in the USSR, were afraid for their position, because at the same time with the Latin alphabet the patriotic-minded national intelligentsia demanded that Moldavian be declared not only the official language in Soviet Moldavia, but also the language of discourse among the republic's nationalities. The meaning of this was that knowing Moldavian would be obligatory for those occupying official (and not only official) positions in Soviet Moldavia. Thus, the substratum of the quarrel with the indigenous population about the status of Moldavian and its alphabet was a matter of vital importance to both the Moldavians and the Russians. Because, if Russian ceased to be the language of discourse among the nationalities of Soviet Moldavia, the Russian inhabitants of this republic would lose their dominant position.

In the final analysis, the Russians in Soviet Moldavia and their supporters gave a hostile reception to demands of vital importance to the overwhelming majority of Moldavians. Thus, for example, publication of the bill *On the transition of the Moldavian language's writing to Latin graphics* stirred up numerous indignant reactions among the activists of the "Unity."[57] "Unity" and its supporters displayed a hostile attitude toward the demands of the Moldavians that immigration into the republic from other territories of the USSR and vice versa be ceased, as well as the emigration of Moldavians (mainly young people) from the republic to remote parts of the country, toward the demands that the falsifications of the republic's obedient historians, sociologists, economists, and so on be exposed.

---

[56]*Narodnoe obrazovanie*, Chişinău, August 13, 1988.

[57]See *Sovetskaia Moldavia*, April 18, 19, 20, 25; May 5, 19, 1989.

INTRODUCTION 37

The harsh contrast between the position of the patriotic-minded majority of the indigenous population and that of the Russians, the Russianized people, and their yes-men of Moldavian extraction clearly appeared during the elections of the Congress of People's Deputies of the USSR from Soviet Moldavia. Despite numerous violations of the election law to the detriment of the candidates who fought for the national aspirations of the indigenous population, seven Moldavian writers, among whom such fearless ones as Grigore Vieru, Leonida Lari (Liubov Iorga), Nicolae Dabija (Ciobanu), Dumitru Matcovschi, were elected people's deputies.

In his speech at the Congress of People's Deputies, Ion Druță underlined that the deputies who were elected to the Congress on the basis of direct suffrage came out of the elections with "wounds and scars."[58] Although he said: "all of us consider the elections over...," there is no doubt that he referred to the kind of elections that took place in Moldavia, and first and foremost to the Moldavian writers who were elected people's deputies. Indeed, in the course of the electoral campaign, the Moldavian writers who were candidates were subjected to malicious attacks, called nationalists, fascists, and were even under the threat of murder. Thus, Vasile Niță, a retired history teacher and head master, declared at a pre-election meeting: "For such a poem (as *Thirteen Verses on Mankurts*[59]) I would have shot Grigore Vieru on the spot."[60] Such aggressiveness is not at all surprising if we take into account the hypocritical policy and duplicity of the leadership of the republic headed by Grossu.

Thus, on 11 May 1989, in his report at a plenary session of the Central Committee of the Moldavian Communist Party, S. Grossu subjected the party's newspapers *Sovetskaia Moldavia*, *Moldova Socialistă*, *Viața Satului* to moderate criticism saying that "they do not reflect opportunely and on the whole the complex political situation in the republic."[61] On the other hand, in his report Grossu

---

[58]*Izvestia*, June 2, 1989.

[59]*Mankurts* — people who lost their ethnic memory.

[60]Vieru, G., "Glontele internaționalist," *Literatura și Arta*, April 6, 1989.

[61]*Literatura și Arta*, May 18, 1989.

attacked in a very strong manner the magazine of the Moldavian writers, *Literatura și Arta*. He asserted that "in this magazine, ideologically and politically harmful publications often appear, provoking people's indignation, stirring the sentiment of national superiority."[62]

The sharp words used against the magazine of the writers on the one hand, and the light reproaches to the party's newspapers on the other hand, testify Grossu's real attitude, since *Sovetskaia Moldavia* and *Moldova Socialistă* were aggressive mouthpieces of the Internationalist front "Unity" and its supporters of both Russian and non-Russian extraction, whereas *Literatura și Arta* courageously fought for the material and spiritual values of the Moldavians. And namely *Sovetskaia Moldavia* resorted to rough falsifications in its attacks against the Moldavian writers's demands concerning the language of the native population, the Latin alphabet, and so on.

In the issue of *Literatura și Arta* with Grossu's report we also find two poems. The author of one of them, Grigore Vieru, writes about the "internationalists" who directly or indirectly share the ideas of "Unity" and "falsify in a provocative way (in Russian) the content of certain decisions of the Moldavian Writers' Union."[63] Vieru's poem is entitled *Inscripție pe stâlpul porții* (*Inscription on the Gate's Bar*). As a warning for the newcomers who detest the Moldavians's "our language and our homeland" ("*al nostru grai, al nostru plai*"), the poet exclaims in the final lines: "*Răbdăm. Dar totul, negreșit/ Pe lume are un sfârșit.*"("We endure. But everything, no doubt/Has an end into this world.")

The second poem entitled *Face to Face* belongs to Leonida Lari. If Vieru rebukes the newcomers for their arrogant and insulting behavior toward the Moldavians and their national patrimony, Lari shoots the arrows at the "*Mankurts*" of Moldavian extraction who play into the hands of the newcomers.

*****

---

[62]Ibid.

[63]Vieru, G., "Inscripție pe stâlpul porții," *Literatura și Arta*, May 18, 1989.

INTRODUCTION 39

In the national press of the republic one can find many striking illustrations of infringements of the election rules to the detriment of the representatives of the Moldavian intelligentsia who had been nominated as candidates to the Supreme Soviet of the USSR.

The fact that, despite all obstacles, seven Moldavian writers were elected people's deputies testifies to the renaissance of the Moldavians's national-ethnic self-consciousness. Meanwhile, the selfless struggle of the national intelligentsia's representatives for the basic rights of the native population and the massive adherence to their great efforts encounter ever stronger resistance not only from the incited Russian-speaking inhabitants, but also from the republic's communist leadership.

The numerous tergiversations in the question of the status of the Moldavian language and its alphabet, the fact that "Unity's" activists give utterance at meetings approved by authorities to openly chauvinistic feelings and cruel abhorrence to patriotic-minded Moldavian intellectuals show that the outcome of the courageous struggle for the basic rights of the Moldavians cannot be predicted yet. There is enough evidence for such statements.

Thus, in a lecture at the Home of Political Education in Chişinău, Nina Gorbanenko, a senior research associate of the History Institute of the Central Committee of the Communist Party, named the Moldavians "*bydlo*" ("the rabble").[64] Or, for example, in a letter filled with coarse invectives, A. Nacu, a "*Mankurt*" of Moldavian extraction, called Mihai Cimpoi (a people's deputy of the USSR) a "provocateur (who), as many others in the local Writers' Union, ...wishes bloodshed in Moldavia."[65]

It was quite clear that now, as in the past, the leadership of the Communist Party of the Soviet Union sympathized with the Russian newcomers in the non-Russian republics in their attempts to maintain there their dominant position. It is precisely this sympathy that explains the following facts.

Thus, on August 1989, at a special sitting of the Presidium of the Supreme Soviet of the USSR, the question under debate was the

---

[64]See "Cronicar" ("Chronicle"), *Literatura şi Arta*, August 3, 1989.

[65]Ibid.

Bill of electoral qualification passed by the Supreme Soviet of the Estonian Soviet Socialist Republic on 8 August 1989. It is worth mentioning here not only that the law adopted by the highest body of state authority of Estonia was not validated by the Presidium of the Supreme Soviet of the USSR, which acted that way in favor of the Russian-speaking newcomers, not in favor of the old residents of the republic; but even of more significance is the definition of Soviet federalism which was formulated at that sitting by Anatolii Lukyanov, the vice-chairman of the Presidium. He asserted that Soviet federalism is based on a two-fold principle. On the one hand, on the principle of mutual relations between the sovereign Soviet republics (and not "between Moscow and each of them," as it is sometimes wrongly maintained, he said), and, on the other hand, on the principle of the Socialist social system.[66] Thus, the Soviet leaders wished to preserve in another form the substance of Article 73 of the Constitution of 1977, which says that the USSR settles "matters of all-Union importance." In other words, they intended to consider Article 76 of the Constitution of the USSR as a worthless matter, which says that a Union republic is a sovereign state.

Moreover, some days after the sitting of the Presidium of the Supreme Soviet, a threatening declaration of the Central Committee of the Communist Party of the Soviet Union on the situation in the Baltic republics was published.[67] The "Declaration" produced a strong negative reaction among the native population, which found expression in letters of people's deputies to Gorbachev.

Despite the complex style of Moscow's declarations and decisions of the time, it became more and more clear that in the sharp conflict between natives and newcomers in the non-Russian Soviet republics the central authorities of the USSR took the latter's part. Thus, the terms "chauvinism," "chauvinistic moods," and so on (which in official documents are referred to as a rule for the Russians's behavior toward the non-Russian indigenous population in the Soviet republics) are used, as always, in mollifying remarks. But such terms as "nationalism," "nationalistic trends," and so on (which

---

[66] TV Moscow, (Vremia), August 16, 1989.

[67] *Pravda*, August 27, 1989.

in official statements are referred to in connection with the representatives of the indigenous population) appear, as in the past, in expressions of severe reproaches.

In an interview published on 29 June 1989 by *Literatura şi Arta*, Leonida Lari said that a group of fifteen deputies from the Moldavian delegation sent a message to the Presidium of the Congress of People's Deputies of the USSR in which they asked that they permit her to take part in the debate, but the Presidium did not give her the floor. In the same issue of this magazine, the speech which she intended to make at the Congress was also published. The main points of her non-pronounced address were the following:

a) Since 1940, falsehood was the supreme argument of power in Soviet Moldavia;

b) The Moldavians formed at that time 70% of the population and the Ukrainians only 9.7%;

c) Bessarabia was dismembered: its northern and southern parts "with ancient historical and cultural centers, fortresses, and cities" that were incorporated into the Ukraine;

d) Official documents testify that in Moldavia they promote a policy which leads to the pauperization of the native population, to an intense emigration of national manpower, to "a mass immigration into the republic from different regions of Russia, the Ukraine, etc;"

e) "The three hundred years of Turkish yoke did not destroy the language of Moldavia, but some decades of stagnation and of cult of power ousted it from all the spheres of social life," etc.[68]

On 31 August 1989 the Supreme Soviet of the republic passed the Bill on the Moldavian language and its alphabet. The act was adopted with a "compromise amendment" saying that both Moldavian and Russian are languages of communication among the republic's nationalities. In her non-pronounced address, Leonida Lari emphasized that "the national cadres of high and middle ranks are in minority" in Soviet Moldavia.[69] Therefore, even if the Moldavians were not in minority, but in majority among the high and middle cadres, the mentioned "compromise amendment" is in detriment of

---

[68]*Literatura şi Arta*, June 29, 1989.

[69]Ibid.

their national language and, ultimately, of their chance of maintenance as an ethnic community. Because, even if only one member of the Council of Ministers, even if only the heads of institutions and enterprises do not know Moldavian, or even if people who do not speak Moldavian are in a very small minority in organizations of any kind, the language of discourse will continue to be Russian and not Moldavian.

Thus, the law on the Moldavian language was not at all satisfactory for the Moldavians. But at the same time it was of indisputably positive importance for them. On the other hand, for the people who do not speak Moldavian, and first of all for the Russian newcomers, the law on the Moldavian language was not only unsatisfactory, but at the same time of negative significance. Moreover, even the curtailment of the sphere of social functions Moldavian has by the law, which says that Russian is also a language of discourse on the territory of the republic, had very dangerous implications from their point of view. This was because, if Moldavian was the official language and at the same time one of the two languages of discourse on the republic's territory, then it could be expected, for example, that one of the next demands of the patriotic-minded Moldavian intellectuals would be that Moldavian be transformed into the number one subject of study both in the Moldavian and in the Russian language elementary schools, into the language of study in the higher schools. Or it could also be expected that one of the next demands would be the knowledge of the official language by those who are eligible for important positions in the Party and governmental bodies of the republic and by those who represent the latter in the Supreme Soviet of the USSR; so that people who did not know the official language of the republic and who were not even its residents, like, let us say, one marshal of the Soviet Union (Sergey Arkhomeev) and two colonel-generals (Ivan Mozorov and Vladimir Osipov) who were people's deputies of the USSR from the Moldavian Soviet Socialist Republic could no longer be elected officials. It is no wonder, therefore, that general strikes of non-Moldavian speaking people began in the main Russianized cities of the republic, such as Tiraspol, Bender, Bălți, Rybnitsa, and, partially, Chișinău many days before the Bill on the status of the Moldavian language was passed, and continued, despite the "compromise amendment," soon after.

It has already been mentioned that subsequent developments in Soviet Moldavia were not predictable. But it was quite clear that, on the one hand, Moscow could no longer rule over the empire as before, and, on the other hand, that the Moldavians (like many other peoples of the USSR) did not want to live as before.

Between the Putsch against Gorbachev and the One against Yeltsin

After Gorbachev's Moscow had removed S. Grossu overnight from his position as first secretary of the Central Committee of the Communist Party of Moldavia, they replaced him with P. Luchinschi, whom they brought from Tadjikistan. The latter failed, though, in his attempt to become, at the same time, president of the parliament of the republic, the deputies electing Mircea Snegur to this position. Shortly after his failure Luchinschi was summoned back to Moscow and introduced in the political office of the Communist Party of the Soviet Union. After the putsch of 1991 he came back to Moldavia, at first being appointed ambassador of the republic in Moscow and, at the end of the year 1992, elected president of the parliament of the Republic of Moldavia in place of professor Alexandru Moşanu who had resigned from this post. Along with Moşanu, three other important members of the parliament also resigned because they opposed the conciliatory attitude of Mircea Snegur, the president of the republic, toward the imperialistic policy promoted by Moscow (Ion Hadârcă, first vice president of the republic; Valeriu Matei and Vasile Nedelciuc, members of the presidium of the parliament). The resignation of the four members of the parliament was a direct consequence of the serious political changes that had taken place in the Republic of Moldavia.

More than half a year before the signing, at Minsk, on 8 December 1991, of the agreement amongst the representatives of Russia (B. Yeltsin), the Ukraine (L. Kravciuc), and Belorussia (S. Suschevici) regarding the creation of the Community of the Independent States (CIS), which formally represented the cessation of the existence of the Soviet Union, the legislative body of Moldavia had changed (on 23 May 1991) the name of the Soviet Socialist Republic of Moldavia to that of the Republic of Moldavia. On 27 August 1991 the parliament of the republic adopted its Declaration of Independence. All this led to greater tension in the political situation. The 14th Army, present on the territory of the republic, played an important role in the extraordinary aggravation of this situation by openly supporting separatist forces on the left bank of the Dniester River who had proclaimed, already on 20 September 1990, the so-called Nistrian-Moldavian Soviet Socialist Republic.

The war that burst out in May 1992, caused by the self-proclaimed Nistrian republic, with the massive participation on its side of Cossack mercenaries recruited from different territories of the former USSR, and of units of the 14th Army, brought about serious casualties and enormous material losses for the Republic of Moldavia. The emissaries sent by Russia to Transnistria, both before the outburst of the hostilities and after their cessation (May-July 1992), demonstrated not only on whose side Russia was in the endless confrontations caused by the separatists from Tiraspol and Comrat, but also that the turbulence in the non-Russian republics were most often purposely instigated by Moscow, whose intention was to reimpose its domination over them, causing discord and conflicts amongst the native and the non-native populations of these republics, called by the promoters of the neo-imperialistic policy "nearby foreign lands" ("*blizhnee zarubeshie*").

The neo-imperialistic policy and practice of Russia were nourished to a great extent by the intensification inside it of the harsh contradictions and the irreconcilable internal struggles between the legislative power and the executive one. Each of them was trying to make the Russians believe (and not only the Russians, but also the multinational population of the Russian federation, as well as the Russophones and the *Mankurts* from the union non-Russian republics) that they were the ones who were defending the vital national interests of the country.

Under these circumstances it is not surprising that each of the divergent political forces were doing their best to prove their "patriotism." But the two camps, both the conservative forces (in fact chauvinistic) gathered around the president of the Russian Parliament, R. Hasbulatov, and the vice president of the Russian Federation, A.

Rutskoi, as well as those called democratic (who are more attenuated in form, but not less imperialistic in content), grouped around Boris Yeltsin, the president of the federation, use the term "patriotism" in the same way that the Soviets used it for decades to cover the imperialistic objectives of Russian chauvinism. For what else could mean, for instance, Yeltsin's declaration in a meeting of the Security Council of the Russian Federation that the "border between Tadjikistan and Afghanistan is a Russian border."[70] Or, for example, Ruţkoi's words uttered in a meeting of the "deputies on all levels" (like in the time of Gorbachev-Luchianov, the last period of existence of the USSR, Hasbulatov-Ruţkoi began to resort to this form of making public opinion believe that the policy promoted by the Supreme Soviet was supported by the whole country): "We need solidarity so that we can recreate the Soviet Union."[71]

The bloodshed in Baku, Tbilisi, Riga, and Vilnius in Gorbachev's time, and that in Abhazia, Moldavia, Northern Oseţia, Inguşeţia, Tadjikistan in Yeltsin's time were directly or indirectly incited both by the legislative as well as by the executive structures of Russia. The goal of the two structures was essentially the same one: on the one hand, to frighten and discourage the patriotic forces of the respective non-Russian republics, who were and still are fighting for their real independence, and, on the other hand, to encourage and stimulate the Russophones, the *Mankurts*, in general all those who are trying to reestablish Russian domination over the former Soviet Empire. By its open or concealed actions, Moscow's neo-imperialistic leadership (regardless of the reformist or conservative orientation of the respective structures of the state powers) managed in this way not only to cause discord amongst the natives of each of the respective non-Russian republics which had declared their independence, but also to bring back to power the former communist leaders (Shevarnadze, Aliev, Karimov, etc.)

In the Republic of Moldavia, the impressive victories of the Popular Front in the years 1989-1990 were undermined to a great extent both by the Russophones and the *Mankurts* inside the front, as

---

[70] TV Moscow, July 27, 1993.

[71] Ibid., September 17, 1993.

well as by the Agrarian Bloc from the parliament of the republic, as they always enjoyed support from the Supreme Soviet and the government of Russia. Both before and after the appearance on the territory of the Republic of Moldavia of the self-proclaimed autonomous Nistrian and Gagaut republics, President Snegur addressed Moscow many times (not only in Gorbachev's time, but also after the collapse of the USSR, in Yeltsin's period) asking for the retreat of its 14th Army from the territory of the republic. But instead of withdrawing its troops, Moscow summoned back (after the bloodshed of May-July 1992) their commander, the aggressive general Netcaciov, and named the more warlike general Alexander Lebed in his place. The latter created real problems for Moscow's leadership by making declarations that divulged the real direction of the policy promoted by the Russian neo-imperialists: for example, he said that the 14th Army would not leave the Nistrian republic because, allegedly, its force was made up in majority of natives.

Although, repeatedly, Lebed did not comply with Moscow's official position, uncovering the true objectives of its pharisaic policy, not only was he kept in his position, but he was also promoted. In 1993 Lieutenant General Lebed also became a deputy in the Supreme Soviet of the self-proclaimed Nistrian republic. Taking into consideration that the president of this republic, I. Smirnov, is also a foreigner like many others there, it can be said, basically, that this is a reiteration of the Soviet *experience* with the formation of the autonomous Moldavian republic on the left bank of the Dniester in 1924. They even named the present Nistrian Republic the "Moldavian" Republic!

In the first years after the Bolsheviks took power, Moscow, trying to get back the territories that had been under Tsarist domination before the revolution of October 1917, created not only the so-called autonomous Soviet Moldavian Republic, but others, such as the autonomous Careliene Republic, for the same reasons, as well. Moscow Television broadcasted a program dedicated especially to this republic. The reporter Portnikov pointed out that the purpose of the creation of the Careliene Republic was to get Finland back. He added that a large proper Russian territory was added to this administrative-political organization just for the eyes of the world.[72]

They operated in the same way when the autonomous Moldavian Republic was created on the territory of the Ukraine in 1924. This time the goal was to retrieve Bessarabia which, at the beginning of 1918, had united with Romania. And also for the eyes of the world, to justify the appearance of the autonomous Moldavian Republic, Moscow enlarged by a lot the territory on which it was created, including in it raions with reduced Moldavian populations even in comparison with that on the left bank of the Dniester, where it was also in minority.

In the above mentioned Moscow television program, V. Stepanov, the president of the Supreme Soviet of the autonomous Republic of Carelia, also spoke. Among other things, Stepanov said that time would soon come when each inhabitant of this republic would declare himself to be Carelian. Not only in Carelia, but also in Moldavia and in other non-Russian republics, the Russophone population tries to substitute the term *native population* with the term *titular population*. This tendency is reflected, for instance, in the constitution adopted in 1978 in Soviet Moldavia, in which it is said that it was adopted by the *people of Moldavia* (not by the *Moldavian people*). The attempt to thus dispossess the representatives of the autochthonous population and to consider them as *part of the people* of the republic is still continuing nowadays. In their overwhelming majority, the Russians, who insist on being considered an *integral part of the people* of this or that national non-Russian republic, do not, nevertheless, renounce their belonging to the *Russian people*. The late professor A. Lisetsky, who died in 1993, in his quality of deputy of the Parliament of the Moldavian Republic, tried to justify the substitution of the term *native nation* with the term *titular nation*, and of the term *the Moldavian people* with the term *the people of Moldavia*, never renounced his belonging to *the Russian people*.

Despite the fact that more than four years have passed since the adoption of the law "Regarding the statute of the state language of the Moldavian Soviet Socialist Republic," the provisions of the article

---

[72]Ibid., September 25, 1993.

which says: "The state language of the Moldavian Soviet Socialist Republic is the Moldavian language. The state language is used in political, economic, social, and cultural life..." are not only disregarded, but also blocked, *de facto*, by important officials in the top forums of the republic.

In this respect, the following declarations of a number of dignitaries in the state Department of Languages are relevant. Thus, Alexandru Bantoş wrote that "by the endeavor of the 'national' nomenclature, the official work language, as it has been until now, still continues to be Russian almost everywhere:"

> "as long as the present governmental structures still teem with people of the yesterday elite, armed with the regrettable ideological arsenal, disguised, it is true, in local patriotism, sovereign and independent, we will continue to flounder in the morass of definitive denationalization."[73]

Alexeii Bogoja, the head of the onomastic department of the Department of Languages, declared that "in 1992 the absolute majority of the students, graduates of the Polytechnic Institute of Chişinău, wrote their thesis in Russian:"

> "the head of a computer center expressed his attitude toward the Romanian language in the following words: *'poka v nashei respublike net nadobnosti izucit' rumânskii. Eto vedi ne agliiskii, ne franţuzskii'* (for the moment there is no need for the studying of the Romanian language in our republic; it is not either English, or French, is it?);"
> "on the one hand, the specialists of the state Department of Languages express their despair because the Romanian language does not function, being dead in its own country, and, on the other hand, all the institutions are 'insistently asked' (in context: through circular a-04128 of January 1992 signed by a deputy minister of the republic — M.B.)

---

[73]A. Bantoş, "Cine trage clopotele la guvern," *Literatura şi Arta*, March 14, 1993.

to write in the Russian language as well." ("Coroana de paie a graiului matern").[74]

In the concrete conditions of the Moldavian Republic (as well as in other non-Russian republics which had proclaimed their independence), the situation was always aggravated by the either outspoken or disguised actions of the neo-imperialist chauvinist forces in Moscow, which caused a continuous worsening of the conflicts between the native patriots, on the one hand, and the Russophones and the *Mankurts*, on the other hand. The latter, being encouraged by the ever more aggressive position of Moscow's legislative structures (especially of the chauvinists within these structures, who were asking that the Soviet Union be restored), were becoming more and more intransigent and impertinent. The reaction of the overwhelming majority of the Russians, the Russophones, and the *Mankurts* to certain formulations in the text elaborated by the parliamentary commission as a draft of the Constitution of the republic is very significant in this respect. Thus, for example, Article 1 (1), which was formulated by the parliamentary commission in the following way: "Moldavia is a national state, sovereign and independent, unique and inseparable," caused the objections of the parliamentary bloc named "Concilierea," who *excluded*, in the version proposed by them, the qualification *national — national* state.[75]

This reaction of the "Concilierea" bloc is even more eloquent as the parliamentary commission itself included in the preamble of the draft the following words: "we, the people of the Moldavian Republic, adopt the text... of the Constitution of the Republic."[76]

Not even this formulation, conciliatory in itself, could pacify those who did not want on any account to renounce the reduction of the natives to the rank of a population to which not even a symbolic right of priority over its own land was recognized.

---

[74]A. Bojoga, "Coroana de paie a graiului matern," *Literatura și Arta*, July 24, 1993.

[75]"Sfatul Țării," March 27, 1993.

[76]Ibid.

The text of Article 14 of the draft Constitution elaborated by the parliamentary commission caused an actual wave of Romanian phobia amongst the overwhelming majority of the Russophones and the *Mankurts*:

> "Article 14 (1). The official language of the Moldavian Republic is the Romanian language."[77]

The "Viața satului" bloc, the speaker of the Russophones and the *Mankurts* in the parliament of the republic, proposed a different formulation of this article:

> "The official language of the Moldavian Republic is the Moldavian language."[78]

In their publication, *Dreptate*, which first appeared in December 1992, the former communists, newly renamed socialists, began a shameful campaign against those who declared that the language of the native population of the republic was Romanian and that in the Constitution it should appear under this name, and not under its contextual synonym — the Moldavian language.

In a long editorial article in *Dreptate* it is claimed that "The variant proposed by the Constitutional commission... will permanently nourish the phobia of the Moldavians toward those with whom they want to forcefully connect them."[79]

These are the words that conclude the respective article, which their authors (most likely Valeriu Senic, the coordinator of the socialist party, and Vasile Stati, the one who, for many years, fought with the so-called "enemies" of the Moldavian language) entitled "The linguistic unity and the right of the people to choose the name of their language." This title, according to which the people supposedly chose the name of the Moldavian language, is as far from the truth as the whole "evidence" supporting the arguments set forth

---

[77] Ibid.

[78] Ibid.

[79] *Dreptate*, no. 7 (9), May 1993.

by those who wrote the article. This is the reason why they needed to attribute to certain Romanian scholars (Mihail Sadoveanu, George Călinescu, Ion Petrovici, Dumitru Caracostea, Alexandru Odobescu, Nicolae Bălcescu, and Ioan Slavici), including those considered by them to be classics of Moldavian literature (Ion Creangă, Mihai Eminescu, Alecu Russo, and Vasile Alecsandri), as well as to a number of western scholars (A. Armbruster, K. Heitmann), a position totally opposed to their conviction that the language of the native population of the Moldavian Republic is Romanian, by reproducing phrases separated from the context or wrongly interpreted.

The appearance, at the end of 1992, of the publication of the "socialists" proves that "something is rotten in the state of Denmark," in the sense that the opportunist policy promoted during the last years by the president of the republic and by his entourage (a policy that led to the dismissal of Mircea Druc from the position of Prime Minister and, finally, to the resignation of four outstanding personalities from the leadership of the parliament, foremost of whom was professor Alexandru Moşanu) paved the way for the furious attacks launched by the people from *Dreptate* against the most gifted protectors of the perennial national values of the native population of the republic, such as the poets Grigore Vieru, Nicolae Dabija, and Leonida Lari and scholars such as Silviu Berejan, Nicolae Mătcaş, Ion Ungureanu, Ion Ţurcanu, Valentin Mândâcanu, and others.

The fact that the authors of the editorial article in *Dreptate* tried to present themselves as scholars is obvious not only from the numberless quotations which they use, but also from the way they entitled the last part of this article, that is "A few theoretical considerations." But the confrontation of the real sense of the quotations (taken from eminent scholars) with the conclusions which the people from *Dreptate* drew on the basis of these quotations proves the complete lack of a scientific basis for these conclusions. For example, reproducing the assertion of the well-known philologist Klaus Heitmann who said that "The Bessarabian and Transnistrian nationalists, despite the consciousness of their ethnic origins, kept speaking about the Moldavian people, about the Moldavian language," the authors of the editorial article concluded: "In fact, K. Heitmann records a generally known truth, confirmed as such by notorious Romanian personalities. In 1941, Dumitru Caracostea remarked: 'The Bessarabian language is *the Moldavian language* of the last century which did not suffer changes due to the common language.'"[80]

Nevertheless, on the one hand, the German scholar emphasized, in fact, by his remark — "despite the conscience of their ethnic origins" — that both the Bessarabian as well as the Transnistrian nationalists were aware of the fact that they were *an integral part of the Romanian people*, and, on the other hand, the Romanian scholar had in view that the term *Moldavian language* is a relative, contextual synonym of the generalizing term *Romanian language*, even if in the concrete circumstances of a certain historical period *the Moldavian language*, as Dumitru Caracostea justly writes, "did not suffer the changes due to the common language."

The juggling with quotations deliberately interpreted in a sense diametrically opposed to their true meaning in the works they are reproduced from is a general characteristic of people like V. Senic, A. Lazarev, V. Smelâh, and other "scholars" who, in the pages of *Dreptate*, resort to the whole arsenal of methods and proceedings which they assimilated during the period when they obtained the dominant titles and positions in the republic's sciences and culture.

In 1965, Klaus Heitmann, in the work from which the quotation chosen by the authors of the article from *Dreptate* was reproduced, considers that the natives east of the Prut are Romanians and that their *language* is an integral part of the Romanian language. Today, in 1993, he continues to assert this, as do the overwhelming majority of the Romanianists in the world, among them Eugen Coşeriu, a Romanian born in Bessarabia, and a generator of new ideas in the world linguistics, as well as the most gifted philologists from the Republic of Moldavia, foremost of whom is Silviu Bejan, the director of the Institute of Linguistics of the Academy of Sciences. An eloquent proof in this respect is the Appeal signed by dozens of "specialists in researching and teaching the Romanian language in universities in Germany, Switzerland, Finland, Russia, and Romania" who participated in the international conference "Romania: Typology. Classification. Characteristics." Among other things, the participants

---

[80] Ibid.

INTRODUCTION 53

Classification. Characteristics." Among other things, the participants in this conference wrote in their appeal the following: "...in Moldavia east of the Prut the people speak *Romanian*, a name which should be made official in the Constitution of the country, in conformity with the scientific and the historical truth, (as well as the name of *Romanians*, which does not mean that the inhabitants of Moldavia cease being Moldavians from a territorial point of view.)"[81]

They demonstrate that the "socialists," using the situation created in the republic as a result of the sometimes ambiguous, sometimes even univocal policy which the leadership of the republic headed by its president used to and continue to promote, are trying, through their journal *Dreptate*, to impose once again on the native population the theories they elaborated when they used to be communists, those "theories" through which, over many decades, they tried to achieve the total bondage of the natives to Moscow by the uprooting of their historical memory in any possible way, by the continuous reduction of the social functions of their native language, and, finally, by their ethnic transformation.

For example, when Gamsahurdia, after he was elected president of Georgia, moved away from Moscow unequivocally, the Kremlin set about to instigate internal conflicts in this republic. The policy promoted by Moscow soon led to the removal of the president elected by the Georgian people and, with the help of Moscow, to his replacement with Shevardnadze as chief of this state which had declared its independence. But, when Shevardnadze, under the influence of the dominant tendencies amongst the native population of Georgia, tried to promote a policy based mainly on national interests, Moscow began to support the Abhazi separatists, providing them with arms and directing their actions of undermining the territorial integrity of the Georgian state. And Shevardnadze, the one who had been brought back to Georgia with the help of the Russians, moved away from Moscow as well, accusing it several times of provoking the Abhazo-Georgian conflict and of providing armament and ammunition to the separatists grouped around V. Arzinba, the president of the Supreme Soviet of Abhazia.

---

[81]*Literatura şi Arta*, April 22, 1993.

However, after the Abhazi forced the Georgian forces to retreat from Suhumi, in October 1993, and, on the other hand, the partisans of Gamsahurdia, almost at the same time, occupied Poti and the surrounding districts, threatening the maintenance of Shevardnadze in his position, the latter was obliged "to go to Canossa." Together with Aliev and Ter-Petrosian, not only did he participate in direct discussions with President Yeltsin in Moscow, but he even declared that Georgia would join the CIS. After all this the Russians suddenly changed their attitude and began to accuse the Abhazi, and not the Georgians, of all the misfortunes of the thousands of refugees from Abhazia. A subdued Georgia will enjoy the help of Moscow in the maintenance of its territorial integrity.

As Shevardnadze had declared not too long ago that Russia was to blame for the fall of the city of Suhumi,[82] but finally bent his head and had to consent to the adherence of Georgia to the CIS, Snegur, who had accused Moscow of supporting the separatists from Tiraspol not only during the bloody events of 1992 from Dubăsari and Tighina, but also before that, finally began to declare that "the non-adherence (of the Republic of Moldavia) to the CIS would be a big mistake and that the signing of the agreement of annexation to it would mean a rectification of this mistake." All this shows that approximately one year before, when the president of the Republic of Moldavia had uttered the words "let us stand by our people," which were interpreted by the local patriots as an expression of his Romanian nationalist sentiments, he was not at all guided by intentions similar to the aspirations of the patriots who wanted to get rid of the dictatorship of Moscow. And when, despite all the pressure exerted on the deputies, despite the fact that the *Mankurts* and the Russophones represented the principal force in the parliament, the motion of adherence to the CIS did not get the necessary number of votes, the president of the republic decreed the organization of new parliamentary elections.

The attitude of the new "triumvirate" (Snegur — Lucinschi — Sangheli) can be explained to a great extent and, in some respects, decisively, through certain biographical "details" of the people on

---

[82] TV Moscow, September 20, 1933.

whom the destinies of the native population in the republic depend. The declarations that Adrian Năstase, the president of the Romanian House of Deputies, made in an interview with Radu Eugeniu Stan, published in *Expres* and republished in *Săptămâna*, which appears in Chișinău, are very significant from this point of view. Answering the remark made by Stan: "President Snegur has often made public anti-Romanian declarations. A famous one is 'We do not want to trade the Russian yoke for the Romanian noose,'" the former Romanian Minister of Foreign Affairs said, among other things, that "all the documents of the intelligence agencies of the former Soviet republics are in Moscow. This, evidently, complicates many of the decisions that are taken in Chișinău."[83] To another question Năstase answered that "in all Bessarabia, two-thirds of the population are Romanians, and the rest are minorities, but in Chișinău and in other big cities the percentage is 50%... This also means mixed marriages, and the education of the children in the Russian language! Even many of the people who have to take political decisions have Russian wives and children who do not speak Romanian."[84] As the documents of the former nomenclature, not only of Moldavia, but also of the other non-Russian republics which had proclaimed their independence, "are in Moscow," the *Mankurts* and the Russophones, primarily the Russians, enjoying the effective support, in many ways, of the neo-imperialists from central Russia, succeeded in re-occupying the key positions in these republics, gradually removing the patriots who had come to power on the eve of the collapse of USSR and immediately after it began to take concrete forms. Sensing that those who were taking the political decisions in Moscow were trying to restore the domination of the Russian people over the whole territory of the former Soviet Empire, the *Mankurts* and the Russophones, and primarily the great majority of Russians in the non-Russian republics were undermining the independence of the latter, facilitating the attempts of the Russian neo-imperialism to enslave the native population in each of these republics.

---

[83]*Săptămâna*, April 30, 1993.

[84]Ibid.

We mentioned above the position of the commander of the Russian 14th Army, General Lebed, who had declared some time before the events that took place in Moscow between 3 and 4 October 1993 that his units would never retreat from the territory of the self-proclaimed Transnistrian Republic. However, after the attempt of Hasbulatov, Ruțkoi, and the other adversaries of Yeltsin who resorted to military force in order to seize power failed, Lebed immediately began to blame others for sending a heavily armed battalion from Transnistria to assist those who fought against the president of Russia and its government.

In general, one can say that already at the time of the putsch of August 1991 the separatists from Tiraspol and Comrat were on the side of the putschists, whose intention was to promote a much harsher policy than that of Gorbachev regarding the methods of governing the Soviet non-Russian republics and of controlling their leadership. On the other hand, the leaderships of the republics were, in general, on the side of Gorbachev and those who supported him against the putschists during that critical period. In the same way, in October 1993, the leadership of the republic was on the side of Yeltsin and the Russian government whose policy, although a neo-imperialist one, aiming at the total submission to Moscow of the former union non-Russian republics, was less aggressive in its forms than the one promoted by the legislative structures grouped around the Hasbulatov-Ruțkoi tandem and the Russian chauvinists who plainly declared that their main goal was to restore the Soviet Union inside the borders previous to its collapse. This time again, the separatists from Tiraspol were not only on the side of the new putschists from Moscow, but they also sent them the "Dniester" battalion and large quantities of armament as help. However, when the anti-presidential forces, nestled in the White House of the Russian parliament, after the attempts to take over by military force the T.V. Ostankino building and the headquarters of the government, were defeated by the troops loyal to President Yeltsin and were obliged to surrender, ardent discussions began in the self-proclaimed Transnistrian republic about who might have ordered the sending of the "Dniester" battalion to Russia to help the putschists overthrow the legitimate president of Russia and its government. During these discussions no one denied the participation of this battalion on the side of the forces which tried

INTRODUCTION 57

to oust Yeltsin,[85] who, by his decree of 21 September 1993, had dissolved the Supreme Soviet. But everyone blamed the others, claiming that it was not them who sent the battalion and the armaments to Moscow.

Thus, for example, sensing that after the defeat suffered by the outspoken chauvinist supporters of the immediate and unconditional restoration of the Soviet Union, he risked, because of his previous numberless bellicose declarations, to be dismissed by the subtler and more reserved Russian neo-imperialists, General Lebed accused the leadership of the self-proclaimed republic of sending the "Dniester" battalion to Moscow. At the same time, he added that he knew nothing about this issue, that he refused any responsibility for the actions of the leaders from Tiraspol, and that he was even ready to leave the Transnistrian Republic for good.[86]

On the other hand, the separatists from Tiraspol also sensed that, following the defeat of Hasbulatov, Ruțkoi, Makașov, and the other initiators and organizers of the putsch of October 1993, they were losing ground, and understood that the Muscovite neo-imperialists, subtler and more reserved, would prefer, under certain conditions, not to allow the dismemberment of the Republic of Moldavia and would renounce, at least temporarily, to support Transnistria and Georgia. In these circumstances, they wasted no time to declare that the famous battalion was recruited from among elements that had participated, indeed, in the Tighina and Dubăsari battles of 1992, but which had long left the Transnistrian Republic and had no connections with it any more.[87]

The worries of the separatists from Tiraspol soon proved to be well-founded. On 19 October 1993, a delegation of the leadership from Chișinău, headed by M. Snegur and A. Sangheli, had a meeting in Moscow with a delegation headed by Cernomârdin, the Prime Minister of Russia. The delegation of the Republic of Moldavia and the Russian delegation signed a series of documents which denoted

---

[85]TV Moscow, October 17, 1993.

[86]Ibid.

[87]Ibid.

words, "to trade the Romanian noose for the Russian yoke," and, on the other hand, that Moscow tried to subdue Moldavia by methods less harsh, in their form, than those resorted to by the outspoken chauvinists from the dissolved Supreme Soviet of the Russian Federation.

The signing, during these negotiations, by the representatives of the two delegations, of an agreement by which 12 common wine factories will be built on the territory of Russia and will receive the raw material from Moldavia, represents, essentially, a first step on the way of, to paraphrase once more Mircea Snegur's words, "standing not by the people" of his forefathers, but by the people of his wife, his children, and his grandchildren. In other words, a first step on the way of throwing again the Russian yoke around his neck and that of the native population of the Republic of Moldavia.

Provided that the intentions of the present leadership from Chişinău will be achieved, the territorial integrity of the Republic of Moldavia (as this "integrity" had been assembled in the middle of the year 1940 out of the mutilated Romanian province of Bessarabia and some districts of the Republic of Moldavia on the left bank of the Dniester, which, in fact, had been dissolved at the same time) will possibly be maintained, despite the separatists from Tiraspol and Comrat.

Even before he came to Moscow with his head bent, Mircea Snegur had given proof several times not only of his sentiments, but also of his intentions. Already in December 1991, when he signed in Alma-Ata the Declaration of the Foundation of the CIS (a declaration which was not ratified by the parliament of the republic), the great majority of the patriots, who played a decisive role in his election as president, realized that from the very beginning he did not meet their expectations. The patriots, who had been convinced supporters of Snegur during the period before the creation of the post of president of the republic, as well as after he was elected to this post, such as, Grigore Vieru, Nicolae Dabija, Leonida Lari, and many other prominent writers, scientists, and scholars, considered in the first years that the hesitations and even the mistakes of the president, to whose election they had made an important contribution, could be explained by his lack of experience as chief of state. In time, however, most of them and especially the ones mentioned above began to openly accuse Snegur of promoting an anti-national policy of paving the way for the transformation of the republic into a colony of the new rulers of Russia.

In a telegram addressed to Mircea Snegur, signed "Grigore Vieru, a former elector," the national poet wrote on 30 July 1993:

"Dear Mister President,
We notice that the plan of moral assassination of certain intellectuals whom you do not like... is being accomplished in a most concrete and resolute way. Famous writers, scientists, political figures, remarkable civil servants, who have no other guilt but the union one, are cruelly and irresponsibly attacked in *Tineretul Moldovei* and *Dreptate*, publications which appear to carry out your wishes. We feel pain not as much from the axe handles which strike the blow, as from edge of the axe which is the leadership of the republic itself..."[88]

The national poet, as an elector who voted for Snegur, considering that the policy promoted by the president and by the people grouped around him, provided it will be imposed definitively (despite the efforts of those patriots who, like Vieru, voted for him, to counteract it) will have disastrous effects for the native population of the republic, goes on warning his former candidate for president: "The dislike, to not say the hate, of the leadership for the intellectuals, and especially the Romanian phobia which the former provoked among the population are unforgivable sins."[89]

A paradoxical fact at first sight, but a very natural one in reality, is that those who before opposed Snegur and whose comrades in ideas and deeds did not vote for him, now began to support and even defend him. Among these can be found editors, as well as authors of *Tineretul Moldovei* and *Dreptate*, that is of those "publications which appear," as Vieru writes, to carry out "the wishes" of the president of the republic. Thus, Snegur became surrounded by groups of

---

[88]*Literatura şi Arta*, August 5, 1993.
[89]Ibid.

troubadours of the Soviet regime who, not too long ago, praised the "historic achievements" in all domains of life under the satrap of Moscow, Ivan Bodiul, and under all the other tyrants who ruled one after another before the almost twenty year "reign" of Bodiul and after it. All these troubadours of yesterday, who were guided for so many years by the will and the direct indications of the Moscow subduer and its despotic leaders in Soviet Moldavia, now put the blame for all misdeeds on those who had to suffer a great deal under that regime because of their non-conformist attitude. Thus, the journal *Dreptate*, mentioned in the telegram of Grigore Vieru addressed the president of the republic, specialized in the deliberate denigration of those outstanding personalities of the intelligentsia who have been the principal defenders of problems of vital importance for the native population of the republic. Thus, V. Senic, the head of the Socialist Party, is one of those who, under the communist regime, obtained their scientific degrees and their material welfare by servilely transplanting in the local land theses and assertions designed after the pattern of the theories elaborated in the center of the Soviet Empire, by presenting a false image of the literary process in the republic, and by praising the policy promoted by the Communist Party in the domain of literature. And this propagator of interests contrary to his people has the insolence to call Grigore Vieru (the one who was often libeled by communist authorities who qualified the powerful patriotic accents of his writings as "nationalist limitations"), in the pages of *Dreptate*, a "former poet," whose "notorious ignorance" convinced him "a long time ago" (namely when Senic was still holding forth the pedantries prepared especially for Soviet Moldavia by the Soviet ideology. — M.B.) that he was "not even literate." More than that, Senic claims in *Dreptate* that Vieru behaved "lowly," that he "begged for mercy," that he "entered very deeply into a terrible, cruel campaign of phobia of the Russians and the Gagauts," that "he barbarously provoked, along with other 'patriots'... the fratricidal war on the Dniester," etc. And after this torrent of flagrant invectives in Soviet-Bolshevik style, the conclusion

INTRODUCTION 61

that follows is a threat from the same arsenal: "The sinister grave... is waiting for you in EVERY village of Bessarabia."[90]

The capital letters printed in the publication of the socialists (EVERY) represent a concrete reflection and a direct consequence of "the hatred and the Romanian phobia provoked amongst the population of the republic by its leadership." (Vieru).

The diatribes published by the editorial staff of *Dreptate* under the generic title "Iuda Iscarioteanul" (all of them probably written by Senic himself or, in any case, under his "care" and under the same Mankurt impulses, with the same pogrom terminology) are also a consequence of the new situation of the republic. This new situation generated the phenomenon by which those who not long ago voted against the present president of the republic, *today* (1992-1993) "seem to carry out his wish."

Living under the regime of ideological terror imposed by the Moscow satraps in Soviet Moldavia, it is not surprising that those intellectuals, who were repeatedly persecuted by the promoters of the communist policy and by their Cerberuses, would sometimes resort to certain stereotype formulas from the ideological arsenal of the ruling party, without renouncing, however, the true objectives of the national cause for which they were continuously militating using the means specific to their respective domain of activity. It was precisely this screen, with which the patriotic intellectuals used to disguise the true message and the true objective of the efforts made by them in order to awake the self-consciousness of the native population of the republic, that the authors of the diatribes published under the generic title "Iuda Iscarioteanul" used. Senic aimed his poisoned arrows at remarkable personalities (all of whom he compared with Judas) such as Ion Hadârcă, Grigore Vieru, Aureliu Busuioc, Ion Vătămanu, Gheorghe Vodă, Valentin Mîndîcanu, Silviu Berejan, and others.[91]

In the journal *Dreptate* edited by V. Senic, scientists and scholars who, being aware that they are Romanians, that their language is Romanian, and that Bessarabia is the land of the ancestors of the Romanian people, do their best to enlighten the native

---

[90]*Dreptate*, no. 7(9), May 1993.

[91]Ibid., no. 6(8), 8(10), 9(11), 10(12), 1993.

population of the Republic of Moldavia, are denigrated and insulted not just in the column "Iuda Iscarioteanul." Not only are the abovementioned personalities attacked and insulted in the pages of *Dreptate* with the strongest epithets from the regrettable arsenal of the Soviet terminology, but also other writers, scholars, and artists who militate for the eternal values of their people and against those factors and phenomena which paved the way for the ethnic transformation of the native population. Among those treated this way in the publication of the Socialists from the Republic of Moldavia are Nicolae Dabija, Alexeii Marinat, Nicolae Mătcaş, Ion Ungureanu, Ion Ţurcanu, and other enlighteners of the Romanians east of the Prut river.

In July 1993 a piece of news from *Dreptate* announced, at "the initiative of the Republican Council of the Moldavian Socialist Party, a meeting of a group of representatives of popular diplomacy with G.S. Maracuţa, the president of Supreme Soviet of the Autonomous Republic of Moldavia." The article goes on to underline that, on the one hand, "the discussion took place in a spirit of understanding and mutual trust," and that, on the other hand, "the parties underlined... the necessity of finding a consensus that could be acceptable for all our peoples."[92]

The discussion with the president of the Supreme Soviet of the self-proclaimed Nistrian republic was also attended to by V. Senic, the head of the Socialist Party, who, together with the representatives of the party that had its headquarters in Chişinău went to Tiraspol to discuss with Maracuţa, and "expressed their profound worry concerning the catastrophal consequences of the tragedy in Bender."[93]

As *Dreptate* had repeatedly accused the leadership in Chişinău for this tragedy and not the one in Tiraspol, it is very clear on whose side, in their new posture as Socialists, were those who had promoted in the past the policy of the Communist Party in Soviet Moldavia.

A Nistrian battalion also participated in the rebellion organized in Moscow on 3-4 October 1993 by Hasbulatov, Ruţkoi, and the other leaders and supporters of the legislative structures of Russia. Despite the fact that the leadership in Tiraspol, after the repression

---

[92] Ibid., no. 10(12), 1993.

[93] Ibid.

of the rebellion by troops loyal to Yeltsin, tried to decline their responsibility in any way, declaring that they did not send the battalion to Moscow, it is very clear, however, that they had always been on the side of the legislative structures of Russia, that is on the side of those Russian forums that were plainly trying to restore the Russian Empire on the entire surface of the former Soviet Union. Besides, this is also proven by the qualifiers "*Soviet, socialist*" from the name given to them to the so-called Nistrian republic.

As the Socialist Party of Moldavia, which in most important matters such as, for instance, the belonging to the Romanian people of the native population of the republic, the language of this population, its ethnic name, its attitude toward Romania and, respectively, toward Russia, etc., guides itself by the postulations and slogans assimilated by its animators during the time of Bodiul and the other satraps of Moscow. It is not surprising that this party, like the leadership of the self-proclaimed Nistrian republic, was closer to the policy and practice of the Russian legislative structures rather than of the executive ones headed by President Yeltsin.

This is why we may say, referring to the participants in the above-mentioned meeting that took place in Tiraspol, that "birds of a feather flock together," in the sense that both Senic, together with the other representatives of the so-called "popular diplomacy," as well as its representatives from Tiraspol were all on the side of those forces from central Russia who were plainly declaring that they wanted to restore the Soviet Union. But, despite the fact that the leadership of the Republic of Moldavia was, and still is, theoretically, against the restoration of the Soviet Empire and for the independence of the republic, that is, in fact, as it has been said before, on the side of the forces grouped around Yeltsin, the Communists from Moldavia, especially in their new posture as Socialists, will not have any reason to be concerned about their fate, even in case that Moldavia, under Yeltsin, will finally succeed to achieve its strategic goals. We may presume as well that the separatists in Tiraspol, despite the participation of the "Dniester" battalion in the attempt to oust Yeltsin and his government, will not be left to their own fate by those whose opponents they were both before the events of 3 and 4 October, as well as during these events. In other words, Moscow will not go so far as to leave them at the absolute discretion of Chişinău even in the case that the leadership of the Republic of Moldavia, headed by President Snegur, will submit without reservation and become again vassals of the Russian imperialism, of an imperialism less aggressive in its form, but not less assiduous and implacable regarding its true tendencies.

Karabah, Abhazia, Transnistria, Crimea, the eastern regions of Ukraine, the Baltic States, the fleet of the Black Sea, and, in general, all the acute conflicts, often flooded with human blood during the Soviet period, the Gorbachev and post-Soviet period, and the Yeltsin era, have provided incontestable evidence that Moscow does not want by any means to accept the tendency of the former Soviet non-Russian peoples to free themselves from its domination, that Moscow provoked and continues to provoke inter-ethnic conflicts in the former Soviet non-Russian territories to be able to impose itself afterwards as a mediator inside the republics affected by former Soviet imperialism and of Russian neo-imperialism of today.

*****

In the speech he made on 26 June 1991 at the opening of the International Conference "The Molotov-Ribbentrop Pact and its Consequences for Bessarabia," Mircea Snegur said, among other things:

a) after "the lands of the Moldavian State were divided up by the hostile and aggressive empires at the end of the eighteenth and the beginning of the nineteenth centuries, there appears, in Southeastern Europe..., 'the problem of Bessarabia and Northern Bucovina';"

b) that "after the First World War... the population of these occupied territories realized its natural right to self-determination and independence, re-establishing historical justice;"

c) that "following their occupation by the Red Army and their inclusion in the Soviet state... the population of Bessarabia, Northern Bucovina, and Herţa District, as well as the peoples of the Baltic States, a foreign state, hostile and incompatible with their ethnic nature, and with their historic and cultural traditions was imposed upon them;"

d) that the political struggle taking place in the republic is carried on, on the one hand, by the forces "that make efforts toward the success of the movement for national liberation, toward the collapse of the cruel and infamous domination under its own burden of sins and crimes," and, on the other hand, forces "that want to maintain us (in the context: the population of the republic) by any means in the totalitarian political system of the USSR, which, for 50 years, pursued a colonial policy of denationalization...."[94]

He went to say that "there cannot be two truths," and that "history is either true and objective, or falsified and distorted."[95]

However, all these statements made by President Snegur in 1991 are in contradiction with the ones he made in 1992-1993 when, being under pressure put upon him by the forces of Soviet neo-imperialism, he became a promotor of the adherence of Moldavia to the CIS, which means, in fact, the subordination to a foreign state, in spirit and intentions, of the Romanians east of the Prut. We may thus say that the position of Mircea Snegur in 1991 naturally integrated in that history which he characterized as "true and objective." However, his present position integrates in that history which he himself called "falsified and distorted." As his present actions are primarily in conformity with the interests of a foreign state, those elements that have been fabricating and distorting the history of the native population for decades are now supporting and praising him. At the same time, as a consequence of this new orientation of the president of the republic, the Snegur-Moşanu-Druc triumvirate, whose policy reflected, in general, the true and objective history of the Romanians east of the Prut and their national interests, dissolved. This is also the explanation for the creation of the Snegur-Lucinschi-Sangheli, all of them former activists from the Moscow nomenclature of the Communist Party of Soviet Moldavia, who were promoting a servile

---

[94]*Facla*, June 28, 1991.
[95]Ibid.

policy which reflected in a falsified and distorted manner the history of the native population of the republic. The policy which this new triumvirate is now promoting does not integrate in the true and especially objective history of the Romanians east of the Prut. A relevant example in this respect is, among other things, the attitude toward the Orthodox Church of Bessarabia. Thus, in contradiction with the historical realities and the norms of the canon law, the Snegur-Lucinschi-Sangheli triumvirate is against the act of the synod of the Romanian Orthodox Church through which the Metropolitanate of Bessarabia was reactivated. Thus it is not surprising that archbishop Vladimir, promoted over night to the rank of Metropolitane of Moldavia by the Russian Orthodox Church, praised "both the government and the president of the republic" who "adopted such an attitude and made such declarations."[96] What the Russian Metropolitane of Moldavia understands by "such an attitude and such declarations" is the support granted by the leadership of the republic to the Russian Orthodox Church which, on 5 October 1992, took the decision to grant independence to "the Orthodox Church of Moldavia in problems of internal administration," in other words to maintain it under the canonical administration of the Russian Orthodox Church.

*****

It is not certain what will finally be the consequences of the policy promoted by the leadership of the Moldavian republic. It is certain, though, that this policy can lead only to a new subjugation of the country, even if in a form different from the previous one, by the Russian Empire which has proved under Yeltsin as well that Moscow's real goal is to impose its domination once again on the peoples which freed themselves from the Soviet yoke. In fact, it is also difficult to say with certitude what will finally become of the new Russian Empire. The attempts of the chauvinist Russian neoimperialists to provoke disorder and inter-ethnic conflicts in the former Union non-Russian republics on the one hand, and, on the

---

[96]*Literatura şi Arta*, June 3, 1993.

other hand, to equalize the rights of the regions belonging to the Russian Federation with those of the autonomous non-Russian republics which are part of the same federation (moreover, to not include in the text of the constitution the term *sovereign* when defining the statute of the autonomous republics, nor their right to self-determination, in other words to return to the famous formula of a unique and indivisible Russia of the Tsarist Empire), all these clearly show what are the tendencies of the Moscow authorities after the events of 3-4 October 1993.

Regardless of the course of the events, it is certain that, not even if Moscow will reach its objectives to restore the Russian Empire, its domination will not be everlasting, as the domination of the Soviet Empire was not everlasting either, despite the fact that the West is lenient toward the attempts by the Russians to impose their domination in the former Union non-Russian republics, considering them to be actions enterprised as part of the sphere of influence of Russia and thus encouraging its expansionist policy, as has happened in history more than once.

PART I

GORBACHEV'S REORGANIZATION AND SOVIET MOLDAVIA

I. ATTEMPTS TO PERPETUATE OLD-FASHIONED SLOGANS:

The Language and National Consciousness of the Romanians East of the Prut River

After the events of 1940, as well as after the war, in the Union republic Moscow continued to support and maintain in key positions its party cadres from the former autonomous republic. The attempts by these cadres to transform the language of the native population, especially its literary form, into a Russian-Moldavian jargon finally failed. But the promoters of Moscow's interests in the Socialist Soviet Republic of Moldavia did not renounce the policy of Russification of the native population by a systematic reduction of the social functions of their language, nor did they give up the defamation of everything that had been done in the fields of culture and language between 1918 and 1940. One of the most important elements of this policy of defamation was the thesis of *the forced Romanianization* of Bessarabia by the authorities during the period 1918-1940. The theme of *the Romanianization of Bessarabia*, put forward by the servile historians of the autonomous republic, was also ubiquitous in the post-war works of Soviet authors in the Union republic. An article from a symposium dedicated to the fiftieth anniversary of the Soviet Socialist Republic of Moldavia is very relevant in this respect. The editor of the collection of symposium papers is S.K. Brysiakin, who is also the author of the respective article. The theses of the author, one of the most active promoters of the national policy of the Soviet authorities, reflect the position elaborated by the historiography of the republic toward the problem of education in Bessarabia between 1918 and 1940. Claiming that T.A. Crăciun and O.G. Andrus, who had examined the problem before him, "convincingly proved the degradation of education in occupied Bessarabia," Brysiakin intended to characterize "education in relation to the political and ideological objectives of the occupants."[1] The epithets "occupied," "occupants," used by both of the authors quoted by Brysiakin, as well as by Brysiakin himself, reflect the *a priori* conception of the servile scientists of the republic when addressing any problem related to Bessarabian realities during the respective period. However, Brysiakin is not only guided by this distorted conception, according to which the *Sfatul Țării* [the National Assembly] is seen as a "treacherous body," the Romanians of the units sent to Bessarabia at the end of the year 1917 are seen as "conquerors," the measures of organizing Bessarabian education are considered *nationalization, Romanianization*.[2] Today, even the most submissive historians have to admit that "the leaders of the *Sfatul Țării* must be known" by the population and that "it is not right to call them instigators."[3]

The Romanianization of Bessarabia, in the sense of the awakening of the national-ethnic self conscience of the native population of the province, began a long time before its annexation by Romania in March (April) 1918. Already during the events that took place inside the Russian Empire after the years 1905-1907 a whole number of patriots dedicated themselves to serving their people by organizing journals and magazines in Bessarabia in their mother tongue. This activity took on large proportions, especially after the revolution of February 1917. A number of Romanians from the Old Kingdom and Transylvania joined the patriotic movement of the

---

[1] S. Brysiakin, "Obshcheobrazovatel'naia shkola v okkupirovannoi Bessarabii. 1918 - 1940." In *Kul'turnoe stroitel'stvo v Sovetskoi Moldavii*. Kishinev, 1974, pp. 157-158.

[2] Ibid., pp. 158-159.

[3] *Sovetskaia Moldavia*, 13 May 1990.

Bessarabians. In fact, they all contributed to the *spiritual Romanianization* of Bessarabia even before the proclamation of the Democratic Republic of Moldavia on 2 December 1917. The *Romanianization* of the Bessarabian school, as part of the spiritual Romanianization of the province, began only after the proclamation of the republic and, especially, after its unification with Romania.

There is an important qualitative difference between the terms *Romanianization* and *Russification* when related to Bessarabia and its native population. The first term reflects a policy which has in view the national revival of the Bessarabian Romanians, and it does not have the extremely negative significance attributed to it in Soviet historiography. On the other hand, the second term reflects a deliberate policy which has in view the transformation of the Bessarabian Romanians into a community totally separate from its people and their gradual assimilation by the dominant nation of the Soviet state. This is the kind of policy which Moscow promoted for decades in the so-called *sovereign* Union republics, praising it as being an internationalist policy, based on friendship among Soviet peoples and denigrating all those who uncovered its true essence and objectives. As all the other authors who praise the policy promoted by the Soviet authorities in the Soviet Socialist Republic of Moldavia while condemning the policy promoted by the Romanian authorities in Bessarabia, S. Brysiakin's weak arguments are based not only on a subjective interpretation of the analyzed facts, but also on their falsification. Thus, Brysiakin claims, for example, that "only the children of the dominant classes were able to attend" middle school in Bessarabia.[4] He also asserts that the authorities were aiming "to assimilate the Moldavian people;"[5] that they were promoting a policy "of national discrimination... of the Moldavian people;"[6] that this policy had "negative consequences for the Moldavian people and its culture;"[7] that "the Moldavian people were deprived of the possibility

---

[4] S. Brysiakin, op. cit., 165.

[5] Ibid., p. 169.

[6] Ibid., p. 172.

[7] Ibid., p. 181.

to create a national intelligentsia and to develop their national culture."[8] All these falsifications are based on the mystification according to which the Moldavians are not Romanians and the Moldavian language is different from the Romanian language. This mystification is even more odious as the mystifiers know, on the one hand, that both Lenin and the editors of the first edition of *The Great Soviet Encyclopedia* (1927) were fully aware that the Bessarabians were Romanians, and, on the other hand, that both the classic authors of the national literature of the Bessarabians, as well as their contemporary writers were all the time conscious that their language was Romanian. After the events of the year 1940, and especially after the end of the war in 1945, among the most determined defenders of the language were Em. Bucov, Gheorghe Bogaci, V. Coroban, and other Bessarabian writers and literary critics who opposed the activity carried on during that period by I. Ceban, with the support of his countrymen from the left side of the Dniester who occupied key positions in the party bodies and press in the republic (S. Țaranov, P. Tereșcenco, G. Ulianov, etc.), an activity with disastrous effects for the language of the Moldavians. What the Bessarabians were able to save was their literary language. In this form, it began to be gradually cleaned of the unnatural, foreign lexical elements and syntactic structures, and finally came to be identical with the Romanian literary language. But in time, the victory of the Bessarabians proved to be a Pyrrhic victory. At the same time with the identification of the literary form of the language of the Bessarabians with the Romanian language, another process was taking place in the republic, namely the systematic expansion, as a result of the policy promoted by the authorities, of the social functions of the Russian language and the continuous reduction of the functions of the language of the native population. Despite this, a whole series of linguists, literary critics, historians, careerist philosophers (Andrei Borș, Tatiana Iliașenco, Andrei Grecul, Vasile Stati, Alexandr Babii, and many others) never ceased to affirm that there is a flourishing and a multilateral development of the Moldavian language. Thus, Vasile Stati, who specialized in fighting "the bourgeois falsifiers of

---

[8] Ibid., p. 183.

the development of the Moldavian language,"[9] insulted in his numerous articles those who affirmed that the language of the Bessarabian Moldavians is Romanian and those who, as he says, maintain that "the Moldavians are not... Moldavians,"[10] although what the Western authors whom he insulted said is that *the Moldavians are Romanians*, and not that they are not Moldavians.

The fact that, even in 1989, Stati received a prize from the Section of Ethnography and Study of Arts of the Academy for his article entitled "The Moldavian language and its enemies" shows that the promoters of the national policy, the ones who undermined the culture and the language of the native population of the republic, do not intend to cease their activities. In the past, although a great number of patriots (writers, scholars, scientists) did everything they could to *at least* protect the literary language from the baneful influence of unilateral bilingualism, they did not venture, under the existent circumstances, to reply to Stati and the other *Mankurts* (as they are called today, a word put into circulation in the USSR by Cinghiz Aitmatov), who were servilely contributing to the Russification of the republic. At the same time with the changes that occurred in the general atmosphere inside the USSR during the last years, the fight for the status of the Moldavian language and for the introduction of the Latin alphabet intensified. In the front ranks of this patriotic struggle were, naturally, writers, scholars, and scientists who did everything they could possibly do to save the values of their people: Ion Druţă, Grigore Vieru, Leonida Lari, Dumitru Matcovschi, Valentin Mândâcanu, Silviu Berejan, Nicolae Dabija, Vladimir Beşleagă, and many others. At the same time, Vasile Stati, Andrei Borş, Ivan Ceban, and other *Mankurts*, promoters of an antinationalist policy, were on the other side, along with Anatolii Lisetsky, Vasilii Iacovlev, I. Blohin, and the other "friends" of the Moldavian people who were trying in any way to maintain their dominant position in the republic. But the situation changed. The

---

[9] Vasile Stati, *Limba Moldovenească şi răuvoitorii ei. Împotriva falsificatorilor burghezi ai dezvoltării limbii moldoveneşti*, Chişinău, 1988.

[10] *Sovetskaia Moldavia*, 13 March, 27 August, 11 November 1986, 26 February, 24 May 1987, etc.

attempts of Stati and the other *Mankurts* to "prove" that the Russian alphabet is more appropriate for the national language than the Latin one, as well as Stati's attacks against the Western authors who observed the lamentable situation of the language of the native population are no more protected from criticism in the republic. During the last years, the anti-nationalist and anti-scientific activity of Stati was criticized many times in the pages of the weekly *Literatura și Arta* and in other national publications. For example, the linguist Vasile Bahnaru writes about Stati: "this great thinker maintains with verbal violence and vehemence that bourgeois ideologists invented the existence of a danger of Russification of the national languages in our country, that during the Soviet period the Moldavian language came to be used in all domains of political, social, economic, and cultural life (???), and that the Moldavian language represents an entity totally separate from the Romanian language." Bahnaru goes on to say: "I will not insist on these fallacies, as our reader is aware of the truth. Avoiding the truth, Vasile Stati does not notice and, moreover, does not even want to notice that the bourgeois ideologists are often right..."[11]

A digression is called for here. First of all, we should mention that the tremendousness of these *fallacies* which Bahnaru is talking about is emphasized by the three question marks he inserted in the text. Secondly, later in the article Stati is characterized by Bahnaru as "a typical representative of scientific dishonesty."[12] Thirdly, despite the drastic riposte given to Stati (which is in total agreement with what I wrote about this "scientist" in my work *The USSR: Language and Realities* (New York, 1988), Bahnaru uses in his article a certain term which only makes Stati's actions look better in the eyes of those whose servile herald he is: the term *bourgeois ideologists*. In reality, the majority of those whom Stati attacks are not "bourgeois ideologists," but simply Western researchers of Soviet realities who write about these problems the way objective data compels them. If we were to take into consideration such a classification of those Westerners who signal out the desperate

---

[11]*Literatura și Arta*, 7 December 1989.

[12]Ibid.

situation of the languages of the non-Russian peoples of the Soviet Empire, namely those whom Stati and the other *Mankurts* vehemently criticized, we should then consider that those Western researchers whom Stati praises — because there are some of these, as well — are not "bourgeois ideologists." This explains the characterization of Western researchers using *class* criteria ("bourgeois ideologists"), which can only serve the interests of the *Mankurts*. Stati (who pretends to be an expert in Marxism-Leninism and a specialist in problems of language and culture) qualified the British philologist Dennis Deletant as being a *bourgeois author* just because he noticed, during his visit in the republic, the dominant position of the Russian language, instead of the Moldavian language. In the same article, Stati characterized H. Hartmann, who wrote in 1978 that "the Moldavian language and the Russian language are the most important means of communication among the Moldavians,"[13] as being "*a famous Western German philologist.*" And this specialist does not care that in the terminological system of Marxism-Leninism the *antonym* of the word *bourgeois* is the word *proletarian*, and that Deletant is not a *bourgeois* author, as Hartmann is not one either.

As in his articles, published not only in the Russian press, but also in the national one, Stati also attacked me "with violence and vehemence," I think that, in order to not be misunderstood, I should insist here on these attacks, or, as a matter of fact, on one of the many invectives which Stati addressed to me during the last years, namely that I am one of those *renegades* who, "to gain their means of subsistence, sell not only themselves, but also the personal opinions they held yesterday."[14]

a) In 1971, the poet Victor Teleucă, as editor of the weekly *Cultura*, sent the director of the Institute of History of the Party, which belonged to the Central Committee of the Moldavian Communist Party, a letter written by O. Cerbeanu in which he accused me of "an obvious disregard of the Leninist texts, of the Leninist terminology, of the work of comrades in Moscow, of the

---

[13]Vasile Stati, "Garmonicheskoe dvuiazychie. Protiv falsifikatorov iasykovykh otnoshenii v Moldavskoi SSR" in *Sovetskaia Moldavia*, 26 February 1987.

[14]*Sovetskaia Moldavia*, 11 November 1986.

methods applied by them in the translation of the works of Karl Marx and Frederich Engels," of "ignoring the theoretical inheritance we have from our great teacher," Lenin. I discussed some of Cerbeanu's articles in my book *O artă dificilă* (Chişinău, 1972, pp. 81-112) and in an article published in the weekly *Cultura* (3 and 10 February 1973). I tried to demonstrate, for example, that Cerbeanu's thesis according to which "V.I. Lenin *developed Marxist theory through his translations* from the works of the founders of scientific communism," is mistaken. I wrote then that "in case that a formula, a thesis, or an idea exposed by the author of the original is old-fashioned, corresponds no more to the level of human knowledge reached in the respective field, the translator has the right and, moreover, the duty to specify this fact in a footnote, and not by modifying the original text, by developing the ideas exposed by the author of the original," that "the translation is a faithful reproduction of the ideas of the original, namely of its content, in an adequate form. That means that, if we consider the *translation as such*, there can be no developing of the ideas of the original." (*O artă dificilă*. p. 93). As I thus denied the thesis according to which Lenin developed Marxist theory through his translations, Cerbeanu, obviously hoping to annihilate me, asked the following caustic question in the above-mentioned letter: "Could it be true that the highly creative work as a translator of V.I. Lenin, a gifted disciple of Karl Marx and Frederich Engels, can be reduced to just "a faithful reproduction of the ideas of the original?"

b) In a report presented during a scientific conference organized by the Institute of History of the Party belonging to the Central Committee of the Moldavian Communist Party in November 1971, analyzing the causes of the multiple deficiencies of the social-political translations which appear in the republic, I concluded that "many of the mistakes which are made in this kind of translations from Russian into Moldavian are the result of the translators's insufficient knowledge of their language, namely the Moldavian language." (See: "Ob osveshchenii problem obshchestvenno-politicheskogo perevoda v respublikanskoi pechati" in *Voprosy istorii kompartii Moldavii. Materialy nauchnoi konferentsii*. Tom. I, Chişinău, 1973, p. 266).

c) In a chapter of the book *Cuvînt despre traduceri* (1968), I mentioned that the textbooks (most of which were translated from

Russian originals) "suffer from a whole series of shortcomings, which diminish their scientific and literary value." (p. 133); that, as the language into which these textbooks were translated was inferior to the language of the original, "the process of assimilation by our students of the material of study" is "handicapped by all the deficiencies of the translation," and that "in the end, besides the efforts which are usually requested for the assimilation of the respective subject," as a result of the deficiencies of the translations, the students need "to make supplementary efforts," which require, naturally, "additional time."(p. 134-135). On the other hand, in the same chapter I concluded that, as the students are obliged to learn the material presented in the textbooks, "in this way they also assimilate many of the shortcomings, mistakes of translation, of the unnatural expressions and constructions, foreign to their native language, which are found in these translations," and "the result is that such elements penetrate the language, distorting it, loading it with lexical material and syntactic constructions that give them the aspect of a garden full of weeds. In this way, many translated textbooks distort the language of the students instead of improving it."(p. 135).

d) Also in 1968 I observed an obvious disproportion between the quality of the translations of artistic literature on the one hand, and that of the socio-political translations and the translations of textbooks of history and humanities on the other hand: "the level of the translations of artistic literature is far superior to the level of other types of translations."(p. 132).

All these were written and published in the SSR of Moldavia and are the basis of the thesis about the *identification* of the literary form of the language of the natives of the republic with the Romanian language and the systematic *degradation* of the spoken form of their language, a thesis which I formulated in the West in my monograph *One Step Back, Two Steps Forward: On the Language Policy of the CPSU in the National Republics. Moldavian: A Look Back, a Survey, and Perspectives, 1924-1980.* (New York, 1982). And all these were also the basis of the symposium over which I presided during the World Congress of Applied Linguistics, and which I entitled "Limbile popoarelor sovietice non-ruse: o reducere treptată a funcțiilor sociale." ("The Languages of the Non-Russian Soviet Peoples: A Gradual Reduction of the Social Functions." (See: Jan den Haese,

Joes Nivette eds., AILA, Brussels, 1984, *Proceedings*, vol. 4, *Symposia*, p. 1629).

I should add two other things to what I have already said in connection with the invective according to which I am a renegade. First of all, as a translator of artistic literature and socio-political texts, as well as the head of a department of the Institute of History of the Party, I tried to contribute as much as possible to the identification of the literary language of the native population of the republic with the literary Romanian language. This allowed me to compare fragments of my translations (without mentioning the name of the translator) with the same fragments from Romanian translations, and to reach the following conclusion: "It is not difficult to notice that we are dealing with different works from the point of view of their artistic value, but similar regarding their language (meaning that, despite all the lexical and syntactic differences, both translations equally integrate in the Romanian national language)." (*One Step Back...*, p. 132-133).

Secondly, despite the fact that I graduated a faculty of *history* and that I collaborated with an institute of *history*, I defended my doctoral dissertation in *philology*, and I did not publish anything on historical themes in Soviet Moldavia, as I did not write in the West on themes which would integrate in the dominant ideology of the country whose citizen I am at present. But all of these facts did not stop Stati from calling me a renegade and from including me in the category of those who, "in order to gain their means of subsistence, sell not only themselves, but also the personal opinions they held yesterday."

Along with other *Mankurts*, Vasile Stati fought until the last moment with those who struggled and finally succeeded to reinstate the true alphabet of the national language — the Latin alphabet. This is obvious from an article that he published in the publication of the Communist Party on 4 May 1990, namely the publication about which Mircea Snegur, then president of the Supreme Soviet of the republic, made the following statement on 25 May 1990: "How long can one bear the ironies of the newspaper *Sovetskaia Moldavia*? Does the Supreme Soviet need such a publication? I think it is high time that we, the deputies, expressed our attitude toward this newspaper and renounced its services."[15]

Moscow named Lucinschi as first secretary of the party after the fight for the language had concluded with the victory of the patriotic forces and after the adoption by the Supreme Soviet of the decisions regarding the status of the language and its alphabet. As a member of the commission for ideology of the Communist Party of the Soviet Union, Lucinschi obviously knew in time about the essence of the Soviet law that was signed by Gorbachev on 24 April 1990 and through which the Russian language was granted the status of an "official language on the territory of the USSR," which is "used as means of international communication."[16]

We have reason to believe that, when he was named prime minister of the republic in November 1989, Lucinschi was aware of the preparations which were taking place in Moscow so that the national languages, including the Moldavian language, would remain "languages for the natives, but not for all the inhabitants of the respective republic."[17] This is the reason why he declared from the very beginning that he favored the laws regarding the language which had been adopted by the Supreme Soviet of the republic before he was sent by Moscow as first secretary of the party. At the same time, though, he categorically declared himself against those who were trying to bring up the problem of Romania's dismemberment of 1940, on the one hand, and that of Bessarabia and the autonomous Moldavian Republic on the left side of the Dniester on the other hand.

The true goals of Lucinschi's activity were also evident in some of the decisions of the party organization of the republic, which were adopted after his failed attempt to become president of the Supreme Soviet as well. Thus, for example, the names of those who took the floor at the plenary session of the Central Committee which took place on 12 May 1990, and which ratified the report subsequently

---

[15]Ibid., 27 May 1990.

[16]Ibid., 8 May 1990.

[17]*Literatura şi Arta*, 24 May 1990.

presented by Lucinschi at the 14th congress of the Moldavian Communist Party, show that they were subjectively chosen by the apparatus in service of the first secretary. Thus, people whose blamable actions were repeatedly referred to in the national press took the floor at that plenary session, among whom we mention A. Zhdanov, F. Angheli, D. Zidu, as well as opportunists like G. Dâgai, M. Deur, V. Kerdivarenco, Andrei Lupan.

The election of Lucinschi in the position of first secretary *by an open vote and without alternative candidates* shows that those who brought him from the Soviet Socialist Republic of Tadjikistan saw that he was protected from another failure like the one he suffered in the Supreme Soviet.[18]

The composition of the Central Committee, which included a great number of *Mankurts* and opportunists (P. Ţîmai, L. Ţurcan, F. Angheli, N. Bondarciuc, V. Iacovlev, A. Zhdanov, G. Tabunşic), as well as that of the Bureau of the Central Committee, which included, among others, A. Lupan and V. Iovv, show which forces supported Lucinschi in his attempt to promote the policy of the party in the republic.[19] A clear indication regarding this policy was the absence of Mircea Snegur, the president of the Supreme Soviet, from the composition of the Bureau of the Central Committee, and the presence among the secretaries of the Central Committee of V. Iovv.

The article published by Stati on 4 May 1990 naturally integrated in the atmosphere of continuous tension caused by the confrontation between the national patriotic forces and the "internationalist" anti-patriotic forces, an atmosphere which was not, neither could it be relieved by the changing of rulers. But, as it was obvious that the fight against the status of the language and of the Latin alphabet fought by the *Mankurts* in the Soviet Socialist Republic of Moldavia no longer enjoyed the help of Moscow (which had decided to change the form of its linguistic policy, but not its essence), Stati modified his course of action. An example of this modification is the above-mentioned article, in which he no longer speaks of the problem of the alphabet, even though he had previously claimed more than once that

---

[18] *Sovetskaia Moldavia*, 19 May 1990.

[19] Ibid., 20 May, 2 June 1990.

the Cyrillic Alphabet in its Russian form was more adequate for the language of the natives than the Latin one. Instead, he expressed his indignation that even in the official press "the national consciousness of the Moldavians, the name of their language, the historical name of their own state" were openly being doubted, saying that thus "gradually, a conceptual (ideological) environment is being created, which *a priori* rejects realities that are scientifically and historically validated."[20] In this way Stati continued to fight against the overwhelming majority of the natives, whose *national consciousness* is reflected, for example, by the title of Grigore Vieru's poem *Limba noastră cea română* (Our Romanian Language).

The Removal of S. Grossu and the Swearing in of P. Lucinschi.

The dramatic changes generated after Chernenko's death by Gorbachev's "Perestroika" (reorganization) do not invalidate what we have said so far. Despite the imminent reunification of Germany; despite the collapse of the East-European communist regimes, which not long before had been at the discretion of the Soviets; despite the withdrawal of Moscow which had to accept the loss, to a great extent, of its influence over the state of affairs in those countries, Gorbachev and his team were not going to renounce the imperialist policy promoted by their predecessors.

* * *

In the last ten days of December 1989, the Romanian people gave a memorable lesson to the whole world. Inspired by the heroic revolt of the youth, the masses won an almost immediate victory over one of the most despotic regimes in the Eastern Europe. It is not unlikely that the Ceaușescu regime would have lasted a while longer had the dictator followed the way proposed by Gorbachev's "Perestroika." But Ceaușescu's attitude during his last years shows that he had no intention of doing so.

---

[20]Ibid., 4 May 1990.

Becoming president, Gorbachev began a severe criticism of the state of affairs that had taken root in the USSR under Leonid Brejnev. The "Perestroika" initiated by Gorbachev consisted, among other things, in revealing numerous falsehoods on which the theories and practices of his predecessors were based. This provoked a chain reaction, leading in most of the East European countries to more serious upheaval than Gorbachev had intended.

During their long career, Gorbachev and the majority of the members of the Political Bureau and of the Secretariat of the Communist Party of the Soviet Union were servile and submissive functionaries of the ruling party. Seen from this point of view, Ceauşescu, who in his youth worked within a party that was driven underground by the Romanian authorities of the time, was a *revolutionary*. As many other East European communists who, due, on the one hand, to Moscow's support and, on the other hand, to the political shortsightedness and the indifference of certain Western leaders, came to power after World War II, Ceauşescu gradually degenerated, finally becoming one of the most tyrannical dictators known in the socialist countries since Stalin. But Gorbachev and all those who were members of the Soviet Political Bureau *were not revolutionaries*, that is they did not intend to change the administrative structures which were rooted in the Soviet state, but were *careerists*. And Gorbachev remained a careerist until after the death of Andropov, when the plenary session of the Central Committee proposed Chernenko for the position of general secretary of the party. When, after Chernenko's death, he became general secretary, Gorbachev also proved to be an opportunist who, "to satisfy his interests, would adopt and apply, according to the circumstances, various opinions and principles. In time, the assurances that, with his coming to power, the actions of the state leaders would correspond to their words which, in turn, would always be based on the truth, soon disappeared almost completely from Gorbachev's vocabulary.

In reality, the solemn formulas of the "reorganization" used by Gorbachev were often in contradiction with each other. Thus, when Gorbachev's interlocutors were communist leaders from non-socialist countries he would emphasize the class interests of the workers. However, in his speeches delivered in front of scholars and businessmen from Western countries he would give priority to universal human values over class interests. There is no doubt that the policy promoted by Gorbachev's team had the anticipated effects in non-socialist countries. In the West, numerous circles of intellectuals and businessmen, as well as many state leaders and especially large masses of young people, fascinated by the spectacular changes taking place in the USSR after the famous plenary session of the ruling party of April 1985, highly praised Gorbachev. On the other hand, the influence of the "Perestroika" policy on the socialist countries was not at all the one expected by Moscow. In these countries, this policy determined a precipitation of the events that led to the overthrow of Gorbachev's bloc comrades and to a thorough shake-up of the ruling parties of those countries.

During the first two congresses of the deputies of the people, Gorbachev declared himself categorically against the abrogation of Article 6 of the Constitution of the Soviet Union, by which the Communist Party was proclaimed the "guiding force of the Soviet society," *the only one* which "defines the line of the internal and foreign policy of the USSR." However, only a few weeks after the conclusion of the second Congress of People's Deputies, at the plenary session of the Central Committee of the party Gorbachev himself proposed that the same article be eliminated from the constitution of the country. Some Western researchers declared that, by making this proposition, Gorbachev proved himself to be a great strategist. But the new metamorphosis of the Soviet leader had a totally different meaning on which we are going to insist.

On 20 March 1990 Soviet television quoted French President Mitterand who had said that "Lithuania is an integral part of the USSR." During the same program, talking about the meeting between Gorbachev and American Senator Edward Kennedy, the newscaster mentioned that the Soviet president answered the senator, who had asked what was going on with Lithuania, that some Western leaders considered that they could resort to military interventions in certain foreign countries and at the same time to protest against actions taken by Soviet leaders in their own countries.

The internal economic, political, and inter-ethnic chaos which was aggravating, endangering the very existence of the immense Soviet Empire within the borders established through the conquests of Tsarist and Stalinist Russia, was forcing Gorbachev's team to concentrate their efforts especially in the direction of saving at least the initial Soviet Empire. This does not mean that the Soviet leader and those who were supporting him ceased any attempt to continue the imperialist policy promoted by all their predecessors.

A close examination of Gorbachev's affirmations and declarations he made in his speeches demonstrate that he was firmly clinging on to the positions established by his predecessors on the international level, and that, when he was forced to back out, he would do it in such a way so that the option of reinstituting Moscow's imperialist policy would not be totally excluded. In 1989, during one of his visits to West Germany and East Germany, Gorbachev, in agreement with the Soviet policy of maintaining the post-war dismemberment of Germany and its people, never used, in his speeches delivered both in West Germany and in East Germany, either the term *Germany* or *the German people*. On 16 July 1990, during a joint press conference with Chancellor Helmut Kohl, the Soviet leader "suddenly remembered" the existence of both the term *Germany* and *the German people*. And not simply *the German people*, but *the great German people,* said Gorbachev during that press conference, had the right to the unification of their country.[21] Gorbachev was forced to admit that the slogans promoted by the Soviets (for instance, according to which, after the postwar dismemberment of Germany, two German nations came into being, a socialist one on the territory of East Germany, and a capitalist one on the territory of West Germany) were absolutely unfounded.

Also in 1990, the same Gorbachev, being asked what his position was in relation to the question of the Japanese territories annexed by the Russians in World War II, territories insistently claimed by the Japanese, he answered promptly: "We do not have land to waste." It is not unlikely that Moscow will finally be forced to give back the territories taken from the Japanese. But no matter how the events will evolve from this point of view, the truth is that the "reorganized" leadership of Soviet Russia was trying to hold on to the conquests of its predecessors.

---

[21]Moscow Television, 16 July 1990.

Even some Soviet intellectuals who supported Gorbachev and tried to present him in a favorable light had to do it with reservation. Thus, for example, being asked during a program of the Moscow television on 24 July 1990 about his attitude toward Gorbachev, the well-known dramatist Mihail Şatrov said, among other things, that he would have many critical observations on Gorbachev's activity and his behavior in different situations.

It is true that under Gorbachev Moscow became less severe regarding its attitude toward the processes that were taking place in the East European countries. Even though Moscow still tried to maintain, to a certain extent, its influence over these countries, today the situation is *in fact* totally different from Brezhnev's time when their sovereignty was mutilated, or from the Stalinist period when they were totally subordinated to Moscow. On the other hand, Gorbachev contributed and continued, after the 28th Congress of the Communist Party of the Soviet Union, to contribute to the destabilization of the situation in the Soviet Union and to the aggravation of inter-ethnic relations within the vast Soviet Empire.

Even some of the most devoted supporters of Gorbachev were complaining that the Communist Party was moving too slowly, being late in adopting its decisions, thus allowing its political adversaries to gain ground in the fight for influence over the masses. But the Soviet leader was actually the most responsible for this state of affairs. Gorbachev himself:

a) totally disregarded the inter-ethnic problems within the USSR at the famous plenary session of April 1985, as well as at the 27th Congress of the Communist Party of the Soviet Union;

b) opposed, as long as he could, the annulment of articles 6 and 7 of the Constitution of the USSR, by which the Communist Party of the Soviet Union was proclaimed the guiding force in Soviet society;

c) repeatedly declared that the members of the Political Bureau were united in their activity and that attempts were made to cause dissension amongst them;

d) he tried for a long time to silence those who would bring up the clauses of the secret German-Soviet agreement of 1939, saying that the original of this agreement was never found either in German archives or in Soviet ones;

e) he tried systematically to stop the creation of the Communist Party of the Federal Republic of Russia.

Regarding these problems, Gorbachev was forced many times to back down, proving dilettantism in some cases, dishonesty or opportunism in others. These "qualities" of Gorbachev, the man and the political leader, are obvious, for example, in the following thesis regarding the attempts of the patriotic forces, supported in different Soviet non-Russian republics by the large masses of the native population, to free their countries from the Moscow dictatorship. Thus, he admitted that under his predecessors such slogans as "friendship of the peoples," "flourishing of cultures and languages," "the Soviet federation — a union of sovereign republics," etc. had nothing in common with reality, that the profound dissatisfaction and the aspiration of the Soviet peoples to be able to decide their own fate were totally justified. But the Soviet peoples, he declared, had not yet lived in a *real* federation, and when the leadership of the USSR would finalize the elaboration of the essence and the structure of such a federation, they would realize that the attempts made by some republics to break-up the USSR were detrimental not only to the Soviet Union as a whole, but also to every Soviet people alone.

The fact that the central television, as well as the majority of the press were systematically presenting not only the events taking place in Moscow, but also the leaders of the national patriotic forces of the republic in a distorted light, proves that the "new agreement of the Union" (*novyi soiuznyi dogovor*), proclaimed by Gorbachev and his supporters, could be nothing else but a new attempt to disguise the imperialist essence of the Soviet state.

Gorbachev intended to perpetuate, even if in a different form adapted to the circumstances of the new epoch, the imperialist policy of his predecessors. In Soviet Moldavia, this policy was reflected for instance by the transferring in November 1989 of P. Lucinschi from Tadjikistan to the Republic of Moldavia where he was named first secretary of the Central Committee of the Moldavian Communist Party, a position previously occupied by Semion Grossu, as well as the transferring of P. Pascar from Moscow to Moldavia where he was named prime minister of the republic. Both Lucinschi and Pascar are natives of Soviet Moldavia. The first was born in the Bessarabian village Rădulenii-Vechi, and the second in the village Stroiești of the

Transnistrian district Râbnița. Both held high positions under Bodiul, Lucinschi being, for a time, secretary of propaganda of the Central Committee of the Moldavian Communist Party, and Pascar a prime minister of the republic. Afterwards they were both transferred to Moscow where Lucinschi worked for many years as assistant to the head of the propaganda department of the Central Committee of the Communist Party of the Soviet Union and, after that, for a few years he held the position of second secretary of the Central Committee of the Communist Party of Tadjikistan, while Pascar worked as deputy of the president of the State Committee for Planning of the USSR. These transfers and re-transfers are undeniable proof that Gorbachev had no intention of renouncing the practice of all his predecessors who would rotate Moscow's servants in the subdued territories, called *sovereign* republics, to save appearances, according to their own interests.

What else could be the meaning of the following events? When Lucinschi's attempt, undoubtedly supported by Gorbachev, to become president of the Supreme Soviet of the republic failed, P. Pascar, who was named in the position of head of the Government of Moldavia a short time after Lucinschi had been transferred from Tadjikistan, sensing that he would not enjoy the support of the republican parliament headed by Mircea Snegur and his vice-president, the poet Hadârcă, resigned.

As Pascar himself admitted, he found himself in Moldavia (after many years of service in Moscow) following a telephone call by which he was asked to occupy there the position of president of the Council of Ministers.[22] It is not hard to imagine who made that call. It is also clear that the person who called had previously consulted Gorbachev's Moscow, and not the parliament of the republic.

It is not at all unlikely that Lucinschi would have left the republic, as Pascar did, had the failure suffered by him with the Supreme Soviet been repeated at the 17th Congress of the republican organization of the party.

Lucinshi managed, after a while, to show his true face. The significant increase in the number of members of the Bureau of the

---

[22]*Sovetskaia Moldavia*, 15 June 1990.

Central Committee, and the formal inclusion among them of the almost octogenarian poet Andrei Lupan, the head of a department of the Medical Institute of Chişinău (E. Popuşoi), the president of the Academy of Sciences of the republic (A. Andrieş), and of some representatives of the workers (S. Baragan, V. Strah, and E. Ciobanu) are very revealing in this respect. At the same time Lucinschi included in the Bureau of the Central Committee many conformists who, like himself, had held high positions in the party bodies during the time of Bodiul or, some of them, in Grossu's time (E. Sobor, I. Guţu, V. Lefter, etc). It is not less significant that D. Nedelcu, the deputy of the president of the Council of Syndicates of the Republic, was also included in the Bureau of the Central Committee, and not the president Grigore Eremei, about whom the patriotic poet Dumitru Matcovschi said: "He is a man who loves his people, a man who knows and understands our pains... He is a leader who knows perfectly well the problems of the republic. Unfortunately, I do not know what forces are trying to remove him from the political life. In my opinion, it is a mistake, a big mistake..."[23]

The new leader of the republican organization of the Communist Party was trying to pose as a devout defender of the national values of the native population and, first of all, of its language. Thus, the Bureau of the Central Committee headed by him "took the initiative" that the day of 31 August, when the law regarding the status of the language and the passing to the Latin alphabet was approved, be considered a holiday — the holiday "Limba noastră" ("Our language").[24]

This initiative was taken during the first working session of the Bureau of the Central Committee, and there is no doubt that its new member Andrei Lupan was also in agreement. It is not unlikely that he was actually the one who inspired this "initiative." On 22 June 1990, the Supreme Soviet of the Soviet Socialist Republic of Moldavia declared the day of 31 August not just a regular holiday (in the USSR in general, and in the Republic of Moldavia in particular

---

[23]*Literatura şi Arta*, 10 May 1990.

[24]*Sovetskaia Moldavia*, 10 June 1990.

there were many holidays which were celebrated at most with a newspaper article!), but a *national holiday*.[25]

Despite the fact that the Supreme Soviet went further than the Bureau of the Central Committee, it would seem that both Lupan and Lucinschi should be praised for their beautiful initiative, and that in this case my writing between quotation marks of the word initiative, as I did before and will do further on, is not at all justified.

The problem is that this "initiative" was taken after 24 April 1990, namely after the adoption of the law "Regarding the languages of the peoples of the USSR," which decreed that "The Russian language is declared official language on the territory of the USSR and used as a means of inter-ethnic communication for the purpose of union among the republics." I emphasized before that Gorbachev was trying to prevent, in any way possible, the imminent disintegration of the Empire which he inherited from his predecessors. The text addressed to the medical deputies which I quoted earlier is one of many proofs that Gorbachev, despite the aureole which some people in the USSR and very many in the West continued to attribute to him, was still guided by "the old imperial mentality in the linguistic policy," a policy leading to "the revival of Stalinist totalitarianism," and to further denationalization and assimilation of the non-Russian Soviet peoples.

The Soviet historian Andrei Lipski, referring to the Soviet-Polish Declaration of April 1987 and to the creation, on its basis, of a bilateral commission of historians, wrote that this commission "practically ceased its activity" because "in a series of major problems, first of all those regarding the revealing of the Katyn crimes, the state interests of the USSR prevailed over the interests of discovering the truth."[26] Lipski goes on to say that "neither did Gorbachev, who visited Poland in July 1988, say the truth about Katyn, which the Polish public awaited... I am convinced that he would have said the truth had it not been for the games of the bureaucrats, had he had on his desk, before his visit, the convincing documents from the Soviet archives." But Gorbachev's behavior in

---

[25]Ibid., 29 June 1990.

[26]*România Liberă*, 1 August 1990.

this case and in other similar ones (some of which were mentioned earlier) does not confirm this affirmation made by Lipski. Not only the apparatus, but also Gorbachev himself was trying in any way to cover the wrongs done by his predecessors to the peoples of neighboring countries, wrongs for which not only they were responsible, but also the people who servilely carried out the criminal orders.

The return of Lucinschi to Moldavia, after an absence of almost 12 years, and especially his appointment as first secretary of the Central Committee in place of Grossu who was dismissed overnight, was also an arbitrary act, which reflects the objective reality of the viability during the years of "Perestroika" of the traditions of governing from a position of great empire. Feeling guilty for his past when he was a servile promoter of both the policy of his boss, Ioan Bodiul, as well as the policy of Brezhnev's Moscow, today Lucinschi claims the following: "I think that what defines a man is not only his past, but also his capacity to lay his past aside, if this is needed, and to begin a new life; and if the man is a leader, his capacity to help the others do it."[27]

It is clear that Lucinschi's words represent a transparent attempt to annihilate somehow the eventual criticisms addressed not only to him, but also to those he was trying to bring to the leadership of the party organization of the republic, regarding their dark past. With all the respect deserved by Dumitru Matcovshi as a courageous defender of the national interests of his people, he was also misled by the hypocritical words of the new first secretary. The poet declared with good reason and in complete agreement with the historical truth that "Cernăuți, Bucovina, and the south of Bessarabia are Moldavian territories. Even more Moldavian than Camenca, Râbnița, Dubăsari." But he was mistaken, at least partially, when, at the same time, he expressed his opinion that "Mircea Snegur, Petru Lucinschi, and Grigore Eremei could resolve this problem."[28]

Grigore Eremei, like Lucinschi, held high positions in the republic under Bodiul as well. The writer Lidia Istrati accused him

---

[27] *Sovetskaia Moldavia*, 21 April 1990.

[28] *Literatura și Arta*, 10 May 1990.

during the 1989 electoral campaign for the Supreme Soviet of the USSR that he was not worthy of representing the people as he had behaved badly during Bodiul's time. However, others, like the well-known folk singer Nicolae Sulac, for instance, adopted an attitude in favor of Eremei, characterizing him as a man who knew how to listen to the opinions of artists and always came to their aid.

Despite the fact that, by his election as first secretary of the Central Committee by the Congress of the party organization of the republic, and not simply by a plenary session of the Central Committee, Lucinschi seems to have secured a privileged position for himself, which none of his predecessors ever held, it is not unlikely that in the end he will find himself in the situation of Grossu, who did not know until the last moment that Gorbachev had decided in a totally arbitrary way to dismiss him from the leadership of the republic. An argument in favor of the fact that Gorbachev decided to have a *political personality* held in reserve whom he could eventually name in Lucinschi's place (as he named Lucinschi in Grossu's position) is the following: despite the fact that Lucinschi and his men decided not to include Eremei in the executive department of the Central Committee of the Moldavian Communist Party, Gorbachev and his men considered that they should include him in the Central Committee of the Communist Party of the Soviet Union.[29]

In world history in general, and in the history of the Romanians in particular, we find many cases where certain men, made governors of their people by foreign powers, subsequently led their nation in a liberation war against those foreign powers. Lucinschi's actions in Moldavia, especially after the failure suffered in his attempt to become the head not only of the communist organization of the republic, but also of its parliament, show that there is a great difference between his words and his deeds, and that he has no intention to contribute to the liberation of the Moldavian people from the foreign oppressive power that brought him to power in the republic.

Lucinschi declared that his "creed as a political man is consolidation and consensus." An example of what "consolidation"

---

[29]*Pravda*, 15 July 1990.

and "consensus" mean for Lucinschi is offered by the decision through which the Central Committee of the Moldavian Communist Party assumed, on 31 May 1990, the right to remove the newspapers *Moldova Socialistă* and *Sovetskaia Moldavia* from under the care of the Supreme Soviet and the Council of Ministers, and to attribute the function of president of the common editorial council of these newspapers to E. Sobor, the secretary for ideology of the Central Committee.[30]

"We do not fight for power," Lucinschi used to say, knowing very well that power continued to be in the hands of those who had brought him back in the republic. "We fight for the confidence of the people."[31] But such arbitrary actions, such as the appropriation of the main newspapers of the republic (be it a *formal* one, because in fact these newspapers had been exclusively subordinated to the Central Committee before as well), show that Lucinchi was trying to maintain, at any price, the power of the Communist Party in the republic. And, with this purpose, he continued to resort to the traditional methods of this party like, for example, the using of servile scientists from the Academy of Sciences of the republic and from the Institute of Social-Political Research of the Central Committee of the Moldavian Communist Party (the former Institute of History of the Party) in the organization of public opinion polls and in the elaboration of their results. Regarding the finding that the press gave voice to more and more calls for the unification of the SSR of Moldavia with Romania, Lucinschi, relying on the data prepared for him by the specialists who conducted the public opinion polls, claimed that "82.5% of those who were questioned gave a certain negative answer. 7.5% favored the unification of the SSR of Moldavia with Romania, and around 9% did not express an opinion."[32]

But the cities (Chişinău, Bălţi) and the districts (Hânceşti, Grigoriopol, Sângerei, and Vulcăneşti) where they performed this

---

[30]*Sovetskaia Moldavia*, 2 June 1990.

[31]*Pravda*, 26 July 1990.

[32]Ibid.

public opinion survey, referred to by the first secretary of the Central Committee as the public opinion of the *people* of Soviet Moldavia, show that they selected territories where the Russophones (as a result of the demographic policy promoted for decades in the republic by the ruling party) form a significant part, and in some places even the dominant part of the population.

Regarding this "trump" of the man who was brought in the republic to promote and defend, first of all, the interests of Moldavia, we should consider the following facts:

a) In the situation existing at that time in the USSR in general and in Soviet Moldavia in particular, such a public opinion survey would have been *truly of the people* of the republic had it been organized and performed by well-intentioned people. The main question should have been: "Do you want your country to become, *de jure* and *de facto*, independent from Moscow and absolutely free to decide its own fate by itself, or do you prefer that it continues to remain within the composition of the USSR?"

b) In Soviet Moldavia, the *real* public opinion *of the people* regarding this matter could only have been established, considering the consequences of Moscow's demographic policy, only by consulting the native population and those who at least know its language.

c) The scientists who organize and perform the questioning of the public opinion, as well as those who will compile the answers must be persons recommended by personalities who, through their activity, have proven both in their past and in the present not only their integrity, but also their courage and love for their people.

This is how these attempts by the first secretary of the Central Committee to mislead the West regarding the Romanians from the Soviet Empire could be contravened.

II. THE PROBLEM OF BESSARABIA AND TRANSNISTRIA

The Roundtables of Lucinschi

In conformity with the electoral system established under Gorbachev, one-third of the Congress of People's Deputies of the USSR (750 deputies out of a total of 2250) was not elected by the population, but by different organizations under the control of the Communist Party, including 100 deputies designated by the Central Committee. The new electoral system was totally different from the Stalinist one. Gorbachev's "Perestroika" completely changed the former system whereby all the deputies were designated by the bodies of the ruling party, the elections being just a fraud. But this new electoral system was created in such a way so that the entry of undesirable candidates among the deputies could be restricted. In the SSR of Moldavia, for instance, the weekly *Literatura și Arta* repeatedly signaled out numerous cases of flagrant violations of the election regulations by the leaders of party bodies from different towns and districts of the republic.

This is a specific phenomenon for the whole Soviet Empire, and not only for Soviet Moldavia. The validation commission had to specify in the report presented to the Congress of People's Deputies of the USSR:

a) that "some candidates had greater possibilities to use the mass media;"

b) that it received protests regarding unjustified refusals to register some candidates;"

c) that "attempts to exert pressure on the voters" took place;

d) that in some circles "the results of the elections were being doubted;"

e) that in letters and declarations addressed to the commission, "some citizens expressed their disagreement concerning the results of the elections."[33]

The fact that the report of the commission contains certain expressions with a quantitative and numerical value "(*in some* electoral districts," "*in some* declarations and protests," "*some* citizens expressed their disagreement...*" etc.) is not at all accidental. The commission resorted in this way to traditional Soviet language of diminution, of disguising the negative phenomenon of Soviet realities.

At the same time with the "Perestroika" declared at the plenary session of April 1985 of the Central Committee of the Communist Party of the Soviet Union, the term *Russia* as a relative, contextual synonym of the terms *RSFSR* and *The Russian Federation (Rossiskaia Federatsia)* began to appear more and more frequently in the Soviet vocabulary. More than that, during the years of the reorganization, the term *Russia* began to be used concomitantly as an *absolute* synonym for *the actual Russia* (with the eastern border along the Ural Mountains and the Volga river) *along with the ancient lands of the peoples subdued by Moscow in the past centuries, which today belong to the Russian Federation.* The more and more frequent usage of the term *Russia* with this meaning in the Soviet language of the last years proves that significant strata of the dominant nation in the USSR are contaminated by chauvinism and that they exert a great influence on the leadership of the state and the Communist Party.

The present Soviet leaders highly praised Khrushchev's successor. Thus, for example, at the 25th Congress of the Communist Party of the Soviet Union in 1976 Edward Shevarnadze declared that the members of the Central Committee had to educate themselves and

---

[33]*Izvestia*, 26 May 1989.

others taking as a model Leonid I. Brezhnev, "the leader of the party and the people, the eminent politician of present times."[34]

It is true that, given the fact that the successes foreseen 8 years ago by the architects of the reorganization had not yet materialized, that the means of subsistence of the population became even more precarious than those during the years, officially called, of stagnation, that the Communist Party was trying in any way to continue to impose its absolute domination in the country, disguised and even open criticisms addressed to Gorbachev began to be heard more and more frequently. However, the fact that, on the one hand, despite the criticisms, the Soviet leader had no intention to renounce disguising the position of president of the state with that of head of the Communist Party of the country, and, on the other hand, that a number of draft bills began to be elaborated to protect him from the lower criticism, proved that, in case the efforts of those who were supporting Gorbachev were successful, a new cult of personality would flourish in the USSR.

Being supported by a whole series of slogans (*glasnost*, *democratization*, *the new political thinking*, etc.), the reorganization proclaimed in 1985 brought about a serious change in the attitude adopted by its promoters toward the Western critics of the realities in the USSR, who not long before had been qualified with the most defamatory epithets in Soviet publications. Thus, for almost a decade after the publication of the book *L'Empire Eclatant* in 1978, its author, Helene Carrere d'Encausse, was abused with the most insulting epithets in the USSR. Even a year after the proclamation of the reorganization, in April 1986, Carrere d'Encausse was accused by an academician from Uzbekistan that she was one of those Western "specialists" and "experts" who were undertaking actions to undermine the Soviet republics in Central Asia.[35] Four years later, however, on February 1990, the author of an interview for the Soviet press did not write, like the Uzbek academician, the words *specialist* and *expert* between quotation marks, referring to Carrere d'Encausse as a professor at the Institute of Political Sciences of Paris, whose

---

[34] *Pravda*, 27 February 1976.

[35] E. Iusupov, "U lzhi nogi korotki," *Literaturnaia Gazeta*, 9 April 1986.

work became "a Bible of the Sovietology" and whose "theses deserve to be taken into consideration."[36]

The language used by Gorbachev and his subjects from the leadership of the republics belonging to the USSR (as long as they continue to remain faithful to Moscow) is very different from the language used during the years before their coming to power. But this renewed language, despite the difference in the expressions used, remains a palliative, under which the true sense of the words and the real intentions of the promoters of the official Soviet policy are hidden. One of the key formulas elaborated under Gorbachev and crystallized in the term *the new political thinking* was that any controversies, litigations, and conflicts both between different states, as well as within a single country could and were supposed to be resolved by dialogue (by negotiations) and not by confrontations (by force). However, in reality, the promoters of the so-called new political thinking resorted to a substitution of terms, because what is actually hidden in their speeches behind the term *dialogue* is in fact a *monologue*. Thus, for example, on 24 April 1990 the Supreme Soviet of the USSR adopted a decision by which the Russian language was decreed the official language of international communication (*mezhatsional'nogo obshchenia*) on the whole territory of the Soviet Union. This decision stipulates that in decisions regarding the functioning of the languages which had been adopted before in the non-Russian Soviet Republics and were not in agreement with the decision of the Supreme Soviet of the USSR, the respective specifications would have to be made. What is in fact intended by these specifications is, for instance, the modification of the law "Regarding the Status of the State Language of the SSR of Moldavia," adopted by the Supreme Soviet of the SSR of Moldavia on 31 August 1989, by which the Constitution of the republic was completed with an article which had the following contents:

> *Article 70.1.* "The state language of the SSR of Moldavia is the Moldavian language. The state language is used in the political, economic, and cultural life and functions on

---

[36]Ibid., 7 February 1990.

the basis of the Latin alphabet... The SSR of Moldavia provides on its territory the necessary conditions for the usage and the development of the Russian language as a communication language between the nations of the USSR, as well as of the languages of the populations of other nationalities."[37]

What is also intended is especially the modification of the decision-law "Regarding the Functioning of the Languages Spoken on the Territory of the SSR of Moldavia," which the Supreme Soviet adopted on 1 September 1989, and which, in Article I, stipulated, among other things, that "the state language, the Moldavian language... performs... the functions of a language of inter-ethnic communication on the territory of the republic;" Article 9 stipulated that "The working language within the government bodies, within the state administration, and the public organizations is the state language, which will be introduced gradually. At the same time translation into the Russian language will be provided;" that "The Language of the secretarial work within the governmental bodies, the state administration, and public organizations is the state language. In case of necessity, the documents will be translated into Russian;" Article 10 stipulated that "The documents of the government bodies, of the state administration, and of the public organizations will be written and adopted in the state language, after which they will be translated into the Russian language."[38]

Essentially, these provisions of the laws regarding the status and functions of the Moldavian language do not differ, for example, from the provisions of the decree "Regarding the Usage of the State Language of the SSR of Lithuania" of 25 February 1989. These provisions of the laws, adopted after a prolonged and exhausting fight of the patriotic forces from the non-Russian Soviet republics, were obstinately opposed when they were being discussed and are still attacked, after their adoption, by the Russophones. The reason for this is that, in conformity with the way these laws are formulated, the

---

[37]V. Bahnaru, "Un moftangiu incurabil," *Literatura și Arta*, 7 September 1989.

[38]Ibid.

Russian language is actually declared a subordinate language on the territory of the non-Russian republic in comparison with the state language, in this case the Moldavian language.

Regarding the *dialogue-monologue* "synonym" present in the language of Moscow and the promoters of its policy in the Soviet non-Russian republics, I will further insist on a report presented in the name of the Bureau of the Central Committee of the Moldavian Communist Party by P.C. Lucinschi as a program of activity three months after he was named in the position of first secretary of the Central Committee. This report, entitled "Regarding the aspects of the reorganization in the republic and the activity of the Moldavian Communist Party in the new circumstances," was published in *Sovetskaia Moldavia*.[39] It can serve as a relevant example of the usage of the term *dialogue* in the sense given to it by the promoters of the so-called new political thinking in the relations with the natives of the Soviet non-Russian republics.

Thus, Lucinschi declared that he was "for a constructive *dialogue* with all public organizations to reach a political consensus, taking into consideration the vital relations, national interests, human rights, the sovereignty of Moldavia," and that "preparations are being made for the organization of a round table meeting in the republic, of a sort of parliament on a public basis," in which "the most complicated problems will be resolved through *dialogue*, through discussions," and that he was "against the irresponsible declarations of some leaders of certain movements, against people who... misinform the population." All these in the context of his rhetorical question: "is such a notion as national interest just within the process of renovation of the Communist Party?" and his answer to it: "Yes, such interests exist, and they are not in contradiction with the general interests of the party, with general human interests. These interests can and must be in harmony — but not in the detriment of the national minorities and of human rights."

Further on Lucinschi said that he did not understand why the problems which were troubling the people "do not become subjects of discussion in symposiums, in theoretical-scientific conferences."

---

[39]*Sovetskaia Moldavia*, 3 March 1990.

And with the same "naivety" he asked his listeners, the members of the Central Committee of the Communist Party and the guests invited to its plenary session: "Why should we not discuss, in a qualified and sincere manner, about such historical events as those in the years 1812, 1918, and 1940. At the same time we should be guided by the following principle: we need the truth not to set people against each other, but to draw from history the conclusions that can help us in the future."

Many of the things said by Lucinchi, which I quoted above, are not only contradictory, but are also incompatible with one another. Thus, what kind of a *dialogue* can be imagined between those who defend the interests of the native population of the SSR of Moldavia and those who claim that these interests are not in contradiction with the general interests of the party? And what kind of a *constructive dialogue* could take place in the republic between those who defend the existence of their nation by ensuring, first of all, a natural development of their national language, and the representatives of a certain minority who consider themselves part of a conquering people which keeps *by force* the land of the natives and persists in opposing any action that could jeopardize its domination in the province taken away by Moscow from the country of the Romanian people, whose component part are the Bessarabians.

We will insist on a single fragment from Lucinschi's report, namely the one in which he suggests the discussion of such "historical events as the years 1812, 1918, and 1940" and declares that the principle that should guide the participants to such discussions should be that *the truth* which will come out should not set people against each other, but help them draw from history the conclusions which can help them in the future. But *the historical truth*, which will definitely come out from *qualified* and *sincere* discussions regarding the events of the years 1812, 1918, and 1940, *will set* those who are trying in any way to perpetuate their domination in the SSR of Moldavia *against* those who are defending the existence of their nation and their inalienable rights.

But the kind of conclusions which Lucinschi was going to draw from the historical events of the past is made clear not only by the spirit of the presentations and discussions at those "scientific conferences" and "round tables" whose preparation he announced in his report, but also by the composition of the group of participants. Thus, the main speakers at these "scientific conferences" and "round tables" were precisely the authors of the *History of the SSR of Moldavia* and of the communist organization of the republic (A. Lazarev, Ia. Kopanschi, V. Isac, V. Platon, E. Istrati, A. Morar, P. Râbalco, and others) which provoked and still provoke the disgust of the patriotic native intelligentsia and of all well-intentioned people, and which is today criticized, formally, even by the party leaders of Soviet Moldavia. And behind the disguise called "constructive dialogue" one could clearly see the intention of the leadership of the republic to continue imposing on the natives the "monologue of the party" in treating the crucial moments in the history of the Bessarabian Romanians. This is proved, for example, by the fact that in the respective institutes of the Academy of sciences and in those of the ruling party the representatives of traditional Soviet historiography continued to hold their key positions. Regarding the events of 1812, as well as those of 1917-1918, and 1940, they still maintain the conclusions promoted by this historiography, namely that:

a) in fact, "the historical act of 1812 was auspicious for the "Moldavian people" and opened the path to prosperity for it;

b) at the end of the year 1917 Soviet Power had been established in Bessarabia and the *Sfatul Țării* (the National Assembly) decided its annexation to Romania arbitrarily, without being empowered by the population of the province;

c) while, on the contrary, in 1940 "the members of the Bessarabian delegation at the session of the Supreme Soviet of the USSR, which adopted the law regarding the creation of the SSR of Moldavia, were elected at meetings of the citizens."[40]

The fact that at those "roundtables" there were scientists who had the courage to openly say, for example, that "in my opinion, the history of Moldavia after 1812 is treated unilaterally, seen from the point of view of Russia's interests" (G. Negru) proves that the patriotic forces of the republic are fighting and will go on fighting for the vital interests of the Bessarabian Romanians.

---

[40]*Sovetskaia Moldavia*, 27 March 1990.

After Lucinschi's swearing in (16 November 1989) and the examination at the "round tables" and "scientific conferences" of such events as those of 1812, 1918, and 1940, the traditional servile historiography of the republic, realizing perfectly what were the real objectives of the "constructive dialogue" advocated by the new party leadership, "reorganized itself," resorting to a shifting of the stresses, but without changing its direction. Thus, for example, at the "roundtable" dedicated to the events of March 1918, the participants *did not insist* on the "magic formula" (which had served for decades as *principal* justification for Moscow's claims over Bessarabia) that at the end of the year 1917 and the beginning of the 1918 Soviet Power was established in Bessarabia. Only one participant at this "round table" mentioned, in short, that regarding Bessarabia the interests of the belligerent powers in World War I cannot be reduced only to the intention "of repressing the Soviet Power on its territory."[41] The stress was this time laid on the Russian-Romanian agreement of 5-9 March 1918, by which Romania, to avoid a Bolshevik invasion, obliged itself to withdraw its troops from Bessarabia in an interval of two months. The participants at this "roundtable" admitted this time that the decision of the *Sfatul Țării* (the National Assembly) of 2 (15) December 1917, by which Bessarabia was declared the Democratic Republic of Moldavia, "corresponded to the aspirations of the Moldavian people" (Ia. Kopanski). But at the same time they characterized the Romanian units, which crossed the Prut river to annihilate the attempts of the Front Section of the "Rumcrod" to take power in Bessarabia, as interventionist troops. A. Lazarev, the author of the slogans fabricated by traditional Soviet historiography, repeated his famous thesis according to which "the invasion of the troops of the Romanian Kingdom on the territory of Bessarabia was the first action of foreign military intervention against Soviet Russia."

Regarding the assertion of Kopanski who admitted, *in conformity with the historical truth*, that by the decision of 2 (15) December 1917 *Sfatul Țării* gave expression to the aspirations of the Bessarabian Romanians, we could make a few objections. First of all,

---

[41]*Sovetskaia Moldavia*, 27 March 1990.

Kopanski emphasized that the Democratic Republic of Moldavia was declared part of the "Russian Federative Democratic Republic" (*Rossiiskoi*), but he "forgot" to mention "a small detail," namely that it was declared an *autonomous* republic within the *Rossiiskoi Federation*.

By characterizing, on the one hand, the Romanian units which crossed the Prut river in December 1917 as *interventionist* troops and their actions on the territory of Bessarabia as "*foreign* military intervention *against Soviet Russia*," and, on the other hand, the actions of the Soviet Government in those circumstances as "support given to the working people of Bessarabia in defending *the revolution and the territorial integrity of the Soviet Republic*,"[42] Lazarev resorted to the old Soviet method of using certain words and phrases with a totally different meaning than the one they have in the common language. For how can one call the entry of Romanian troops in Bessarabia at the end of the year 1917 a *foreign military intervention* without deviating from the meaning that these words have in the common language? Even if this action was carried out without the consent of the *Sfatul Țării*, it cannot be characterized as a *foreign* military intervention, as *the Romanian soldiers entered then on their ancestors's land, taken away from their country, along with their brothers, by Tsarist Russia*. And how can one call the actions of the Bolshevik Government and its military forces (and not only military) as "support given to the working people of Bessarabia in defending *the territorial integrity of the Soviet Republic*" without deviating again from the real sense of the words? For one cannot talk about a defending of the territorial integrity of the Soviet Republic (in the context of *Soviet Russia*) after the events that took place in Bessarabia after 2 (15) December 1917, especially after the entering of the Romanian troops, because:

a) The "small detail" which Ia. Kopanski omitted to mention in his speech has a capital importance for a just evaluation of the events discussed at the "round table": the Democratic Republic of Moldavia was not proclaimed by the *Sfatul Țării* as *an integral part of Russia*, but as an autonomous republic within a federation, called *Rossiiskaia*

---

[42] Ibid.

Federatsia (the Russian Federation). As the authorities of this *autonomous republic* gave expression by its proclamation to the aspirations of the Moldavian people, they had the right to ask the brothers of the Bessarabian Romanians (of the Moldavian people) to help them against the attempts of the Front Section of the "Rumcrod," sent from Odessa, to take power in Bessarabia.

b) The characterization of the actions of the "Rumcrod" (which in the period of the events under discussion was promoting the policy of the Soviet Government) as "support given to the working people of Bessarabia" does not reflect the objective reality either. The Front Section (*Frontotdel*) sent by the "Rumcrod" from Odessa did not succeed in taking power in Bessarabia. Even if it had succeeded in doing so on 28 December 1917 when it arrived in Chişinău, or during the following days, this could not have served as a justification for the claims which Moscow had over the territory between the Prut and the Dniester rivers, as on 2 (15) December this territory had been proclaimed an autonomous republic, on 24 January 1918 an "independent and autonomous republic, having the right to decide its own future," and, finally, on 27 March (9 April) 1918 united with the Romanian state. The second Congress of the Soviets, which began on 25 October 1917, solemnly declared that Soviet Power would "ensure the real right to self-determination for all the nations which populate Russia."[43]

All these prove that the dispatch of the Front Section of the "Rumcrod" from Odessa to Bessarabia at the end of the year 1917 was a *failed attempt at military intervention by Soviet Russia* against a former outlying part of the Tsarist Empire which had been proclaimed an *autonomous national republic*. Therefore, this republic had every right not only to separate on 27 March 1918 from the Soviet Russian Federation, but also to unite with Romania.

I. Bobeico, another participant at the "roundtable," mentioning, among other things, that "On 18 February (1918) an offensive plan of the units of the Red Army in the direction of Iaşi was approved," quoted in this context the text of a telegram sent to Lenin and Trotsky on 15 March 1918 by Cristian Rakovski. As this historical document

---

[43] V. Lenin, *Opere complete*, vol. 35, p. 11.

is very important for the elucidation of the events of March 1918, I will reproduce here the whole text quoted by I. Bobeico:

"Arrived with the mission to drive away the Romanian counter-revolutionary forces from Bessarabia and to generate a revolutionary movement in Romania, I was forced, as a result of the disastrous situation which was present also in the south because of the Austrian-German-Ukrainian offensive, to stop half-way and accept the signing of a peace treaty with Romania, which will ensure our maintaining Bessarabia."[44]

Cristian Racovski, the revolutionary of Bulgarian origin whom Bobeico calls "a Romanian social-democrat," cannot be presented as such in the given context. Despite the fact that he activated for many years in Romania and was a member of the leadership of the Social Democratic Party, during the events of 1917 this party, regarding the actions of the group led by Rakovski in Odessa, declared that they "were not in accord with the past and the present policy of the Romanian social-democracy." Especially after the Bolshevik revolution, considering the agreement of 5-9 March 1918 signed by Rakovski in his position of head of the delegation of the Bolshevik Government at the Soviet-Romanian negotiations, it is not at all natural to call him a "Romanian social-democrat," but rather a "Soviet social-democrat" or, more appropriately in that context, "the Soviet representative."

The way Racovski formulated his telegram proves that he knew very well that Soviet Power *had not been established* in Bessarabia either at the end of the year 1917, or in January-March 1918. This is why he reported to Lenin and Trotsky that he had arrived in Bessarabia "with the mission to drive away the Romanian *counter-revolutionary* forces" and not the Romanian *interventionist* forces, and that, because of the disastrous situation, he was forced to accept "the signing — as he says — of a peace treaty with Romania, which will ensure our *maintaining* of Bessarabia," and not which will "secure *the reestablishment* of the Soviet Power in Bessarabia."

The text of Racovski's telegram debunks not only the myth according to which the Soviet power was established in Bessarabia on

---

[44] *Sovetskaia Moldavia*, 27 March 1990.

1 (14) January 1918, but also the one which said that by the agreement signed by Averescu on 5-9 March 1918, Romania recognized the righteousness of the Soviet position regarding the problem of Bessarabia.

Racovski's telegram is of interest from another point of view as well, that is the real cause which forced the Romanian state to sign the agreement of 5-9 March 1918. In this respect we have to consider first of all the Soviet offensive plan against Iași approved on *18 January 1918* (mentioned By I. Bobeico in his speech at the "round table") and, secondly, the intention of the Soviets "to generate a revolutionary movement in Romania" (mentioned in Racovski's telegram). Averescu signed the agreement of *5-9 March 1918* to cope with this imminent danger for the very existence of Romania as an independent state, and not because he considered that the claims of the Soviets were justified.

What we have said so far shows in what way the participants at the "roundtables" were "reorganized" and what kind of a "constructive dialogue" the party leadership headed by Lucinschi expected.

Obedient Historiography in Search of New Formulas to Justify the Traditional Position of Moscow

The term *prisoedinenie* has two meanings in Russian:

1. a derivative of the transitive verb *prisoedinit' - prisoediniat'* = *to incorporate, to annex*;

2. a derivative of the reflexive verb *prisoedinit'sia - prisoediniat'sia* = *to join, to unite*;

This homonym was the main cause of the introduction of this term in Soviet historiography with the role of the exclusive term for the expression of the historical reality of the dividing of Moldavia in 1812 through the incorporation by the Russian Empire of the territory between the Prut and the Dniester Rivers. Thus, for example, V. Tomuleț, a professor at the university of Chișinău (the department of Soviet history, headed by A. Lisetsky) published in 1987 an article dedicated to the commemoration of 175 years from the events of 1812. Using the term *prisoedinenie* in the subtitle, he entitled his article "On a Reciprocally Advantageous Basis." More than that, in his article V. Tomuleț says: "*The unification* with Russia (*edinenie s Rossiei*) had a great progressive importance."[45]

Tomuleț wrote this despite the fact that already in the past decades in the SSR of Moldavia appeared works whose authors, although they were also saying that the events of 1812 were favorable to Bessarabia's progress, they emphasized at the same time that "one of the most important problems of Russia's foreign policy in the second half of the eighteenth century was the fight for obtaining a passage to the Black Sea" and that "the policy of the Russian tsarism regarding the 'Eastern problem' was undoubtedly an aggressive policy."[46] Some works pointed out that public health in Bessarabia was terrible, that "in the years 1813-1822, 1824-1825, 1828-1830, 1834, 1847-1848, 1853, 1855-1856, 1866 epidemics of pestilence, cholera, and typhus swept over the whole region, killing thousands of people."[47] Even the most servile Soviet authors were writing at that time regarding, for instance, the Russian-Turkish War (1735-1739), that "Russia did not venture to take Moldavia away from Turkey (in the context: the Principality of Moldavia) because it tried to avoid a conflict with Austria."[48] Some Soviet authors did not conceal the fact that "at that time (1807) Tsarist Russia was claiming only the Danubian Principalities. This was its principal goal also in the spring of 1808, when negotiations took place in Saint Petersburg regarding the great partition of the Ottoman Empire."[49]

Other Soviet authors denied, however, Russia's true intentions to occupy not only the territory between the Prut and the Dniester

---

[45]V. Tomuleț, "Na vzaimovygodnoi osnove." *Sovetskaia Moldavia*, 7 May 1987.

[46]I. Semenova, *Russko-moldavskoe boevoe sodruzhestvo. 1787-1791*. Kishinev, 1968, pp. 5-6.

[47]I. Antsupov, *Gosudarstvennaia derevnia Bessarabuu v XIX veke. 1812-1870*. Kishinev, 1966, p. 24.

[48]N. Mokhov, *Ocheri istorii moldavsko-russko-ukrainskikh sviazei (s drevnikh vremen do nachala XIX v.)*. Kishinev, 1961, p. 144.

[49]A. Narochitsky, P. Kazakov, "K istorii vostochnogo voprosa. (O tseliakh Rossii i Frantsii na Balkanakh v 1807-1808 gg.), in *Novaia i noveishaia istoria*, no. 6, 1969, p. 66.

Rivers, and even not only the whole Principality of Moldavia, but both of the Danubian Principalities.[50] They did this to create the myth according to which the Moldavians on the left side of the Prut River wanted to free themselves from the unbearable yoke of the pagan Turks and to become subjects of the Orthodox Russia. Thus, in 1960 one of the philosophers of the SSR of Moldavia was claiming, in flagrant contradiction with the truth, that "The unification of Bessarabia with Russia in 1812 had positive consequences for the development of Moldavian culture."[51] In the same year, the historian N. Mokhov tried to contribute to the creation of the myth that "a part of Moldavia, later called Bessarabia, was freed from this yoke (the Turkish yoke) by uniting with Russia."[52]

Half a year after the proclamation of Gorbachev's "reorganization," in September 1985, the stereotype of "liberation" and "unification" appears in an encyclopedia article signed by literary historians from the Academy of Sciences of the republic:

"In 1812, the eastern part of Moldavia (Bessarabia) was freed from the Turkish yoke and united with Russia, while the Principality of Moldavia continued to remain under Ottoman oppression."[53]

Despite the ambiguity of the formula chosen, with the purpose of dissimulating somehow the dismemberment of the Principality of Moldavia committed by Russia (*"the eastern part of Moldavia (Bessarabia) was freed from the Turkish yoke;" "the principality of Moldavia continued to remain under Ottoman oppression"*), there is no doubt that the authors of this formula were guided by the theses elaborated by the historiography of the republic. The literary historians were forced to resort to such ways of expression because of the inevitable discrepancy which existed and continues to exist between the description by the scientists of the republic of the

---

[50] I. Dostian, *Rossia i balkanskii vopros. Iz istorii russko-balkanskikh politicheskikh sviasei v pervoi treti XIX v.* Moscow, 1972, pp. 72-73.

[51] A. Babii, "O temă vastă şi actuală", in *Moldova Socialistă*, 25 August 1960.

[52] N. Mokhov, "O dată importantă în istoria norodului moldovenesc," in *Moldova Socialistă*, 26 July 1960.

[53] "Literatura şi Arta Moldovei." *Encyclopedia.* vol. 1, 1985, p. 392.

historical (political, socio-economic, national) process on the one hand, and of the literary (cultural, spiritual, linguistic) process on the other hand, both before and especially after the events of 1812.

Ambiguities in the evaluation of the processes and phenomena related in one way or another to the events of 1812 were used in fact, and continue to be used by specialists in every domain, including history. Thus, for example, Petru Lucinschi, the initiator of the "roundtables" in the republic, wrote in 1974, regarding the Treaty of Luck and the diploma granted, on its basis, by Peter the Great to the Moldavian prince Dimitrie Cantemir, that the materialization of the provisions of this treaty would have led "to the liberation of the country from the Turkish yoke a hundred years before it actually took place."[54] It is obvious that in Lucinschi's text the word *country* appears as a synonym for the Principality of Moldavia and, concomitantly, as a synonym for the territory between the Prut and the Dniester Rivers.

One can notice a distinctive difference in the usage of the term *Moldavia* in formulations which define various aspects of the situation in the province between the Prut and the Dniester before the events of 1917 depending on the specialty of the one who uses it. In the works of historians, in connection with the period mentioned above, the term is used *in most cases* as a contextual synonym for Bessarabia and *in some cases* also as a contextual synonym for the Principality of Moldavia as a whole. On the contrary, in the works of linguists and literary historians the term is related *in most cases* to the Principality of Moldavia as a whole (or to the territory between the Carpathians and the Prut) and *in some cases* to Bessarabia. This phenomenon can be explained by the atmosphere which was suffocating the developing of the language, the literature, and the culture of the native population of Bessarabia during the period from 1812 to 1917, and by the continuous degradation of these constructive elements of the ethnic-national being of the Bessarabian Romanians under Russian domination. On the other hand, it can also be explained by the natural development and even the flourishing of the

---

[54]Petru Lucinschi, "D. Cantemir uchnyi i patriot," in *Voprosy istorii*, no. 10, 1973, p. 36.

language, literature, and culture of the Romanians from western Moldavia, despite the fact that after 1812 it remained, for a time, under Turkish rule.

This phenomenon could also be noticed after Gorbachev came to power, and continued to appear after Moscow dismissed S. Grossu and named Petru Lucinschi in his place. The essential change that took place already during the last years of Grossu's rule in the presentation of the events connected to the events of 1812 is that even the most servile historians from the SSR of Moldavia ceased to characterize the incorporation of the territory between the Prut and the Dniester Rivers by the Russian Empire as the *liberation* of this territory and its population. The historians V. Zhukov and N. Babilunga, who along with the others used to support the thesis of Bessarabia's *liberation* in 1812, talk now about the "justness of the conception elaborated by the historiography of the republic on the 'incorporation (*prisoedinenia*) and *not the voluntary unification*' of the territory between the Prut and the Dniester with Tsarist Russia."[55] Changing the form in which they now present the *incorporation* of Bessarabia, Zhukov and Babilunga did not modify the interpretation of its *essence*, continuing to distort it. The new thesis maintains that what happened after the Russian-Turkish War of 1806-1812 was not an *annexation* of the territory between the Prut and the Dniester, nor a dismemberment of the Principality of Moldavia, but only a "narrowing of the borders of the Ottoman Empire which was forced to cede a part of the territory of the Principality of Moldavia that was under Ottoman rule," and that, consequently, "there did not take place a subjugation of the Moldavian people, against whom the Russian state never waged war."[56]

A review published by the magazine of the Communist Party of the SSR of Moldavia says that A. Roman, the author of a monograph on the participation of the working people of the SSR of Moldavia in the activity of the Soviets, pointed out that "the occupation of Bessarabia by the troops of the Romanian Kingdom, the restricted

---

[55]V. Zhukov, N. Babilunga, "Chem dannaia veshch' stala teper'," in *Sovetskaia Moldavia*, 21 April 1990.

[56]Ibid.

territory of Moldavia on the left side of the Dniester, and the small number of the population determined, in the mid-1920s, the creation of its statehood under the form of an autonomous Soviet republic."[57] If we leave aside the arbitrary usage of the terms *the occupation of Bessarabia, Moldavia, statehood* on the one hand, and its arbitrary style on the other hand, we can say that this thesis reflects, to a certain extent, the real state of affairs. But only to a certain extent, because the attempts of *Bolshevik Russia* to regain the territory taken away from the Principality of Moldavia by *Tsarist Russia* in 1812 was *the only cause* of the formation in 1924, on the territory of the Ukraine, following the failure of the Russian-Romanian negotiations in Vienna, of the simulacrum of statehood of the Moldavians on the left bank of the Dniester River.

Other authors continue even today to emphasize the "aspirations of self-determination" of the Moldavians. A. Repida, for example, wrote at the end of the year 1979 that "the general aspiration of the people of Moldavia to create their own republic," which was expressed in 1923 by "C. I. Kotocsky in a conversation with M.V. Frunze and S.M. Bydennyi," finally led to the adoption on 29 July 1924 of the decision of the Political Bureau of the Central Committee of the Russian Communist Party, "Regarding the SSR of Moldavia," which said: "The separation of the Moldavian population into an autonomous republic within the SSR of the Ukraine... is considered necessary..."[58] In an encyclopedia article, Repida declared that "in 1923 G.I. Kotovsky informed M.V. Frunze about the general endeavor of the working people to have an autonomous Soviet republic," that "G.I Kotovsky, P. Tcacenco, and other influential communists form Moldavia addressed a letter to the Central Committee of the Russian Communist Party and the Central Committee of the Ukrainian Communist Party in which they were asking, in the name of the people, for the creation of the SSR of

---

[57] *Comunistul Moldovei*, no. 2, 1983, p. 93.

[58] Ibid., no. 10, 1979, p. 11.

Moldavia."[59] I will again leave aside the arbitrary terminology (the people of *Moldavia*). I will mention though the unnatural formulation *the separation into*, which is also mistaken, because the meaning of the respective word in the Russian original, from which the text quoted above was translated, is not *separation*, but *constitution*. What needs to be pointed out is that the specialists in the problem of the formation of the autonomous Moldavian Republic insist, in flagrant contradiction with the historical facts, that this republic came into being through the initiative of the Moldavians on the left side of the Dniester. In reality, though, it is very significant that the preparations for the creation of a simulacrum of statehood for the Transnistrian Moldavians were being made especially during the months precursory to the Vienna conference and that, at the beginning, it was a matter of "constituting an autonomous region within the SSR of the Ukraine,"[60] and not an *autonomous republic*. This proves that the USSR was trying to find alternatives for a possible failure of its attempts to force Romania through negotiations to give up Bessarabia.

---

[59] A. Repida, V. Roshko, "Obrazovanie Moldavskoi ASSR," in *Moldavskai Sovetskaia Entsiklopedia* (MSE), 1979, p. 119.

[60] A. Repida, V. Rozhko, op. cit.

III. DEBATES IN THE SUPREME SOVIET ON THE MOLOTOV-RIBBENTROP PACT

Recognition of the Existence of the Additional Secret Protocol

In June 1989, at the first Congress of the Soviet of the Deputies of the People of the USSR elected in conformity with the principles elaborated by Gorbachev, heated discussions began regarding the Soviet-German Non-Aggression Treaty and especially the secret protocol of 23 August 1939. Gorbachev tried to suppress this acute problem in the relations between Moscow and the republics subjugated by Stalin in 1940.

Seeing that his attempts were met by the firm opposition of some deputies, especially from the Baltic republics, the Soviet leader resorted to a forced argument, declaring that the respective document did not exist in the Soviet archives. And, to convince the deputies that the Congress could not take any decision in that matter, Gorbachev added that during a meeting with West German Chancellor Helmut Khol he asked the latter whether the German archives possessed the original of that protocol, and Kohl answered that only one copy existed in Germany.

As all the efforts to suppress the question of the secret protocol were unsuccessful, they decided upon the creation of a special commission headed by A. Iacovlev, at that time a member of the Political Bureau of the Central Committee of the Communist Party of the Soviet Union, which was supposed to examine and evaluate from a political point of view the juridical Soviet-German Non-Aggression Treaty of 23 August 1939. Half a year later, on 23 December 1989, at the afternoon meeting of the second Congress of the Soviet of the Deputies of the People of the USSR, A. Iacovlev presented the conclusions of the commission:

a) the secret additional protocol of 23 August 1939 existed, although the original was not found in the Soviet archives, nor in the German ones;

b) from a juridical point of view, the protocol was from the beginning an illegal act;

c) Stalin carried out the reannexation of Bessarabia to the (Soviet) Union and the reestablishment of Soviet Power in the Baltic Republics in an imperialist manner.

To this categoric criticism against the imperialist policy of Moscow, which left its permanent marks on the additional secret protocol of 23 August 1939 that stipulated "the possibility of introducing (Soviet) troops in the Baltic States, in Poland and Bessarabia, and, eventually, even in Finland,"[61] Iacovlev considered it appropriate to add that in opposition to the unanimous evaluation of the secret protocol by the members of the commission, there were differences of opinions regarding the Soviet-German treaty itself, some members maintaining that "in the circumstances of that time it was a legal treaty from a political point of view."

Having these reservations, the commission undoubtedly took into consideration and tried to attenuate somewhat the eventual undesirable consequences (from the point of view of Kremlin) of the criticisms of the additional secret protocol of 23 August 1939 on the internal situation and inter-ethnic relations within the USSR. Despite all these, during the debates on the report presented by Iacovlev, and especially when the draft decision elaborated by the commission was presented to a vote, it once again became evident that the declaration made by deputy Iury Afanasiev at the beginning of the proceedings of the first Congress of People's Deputies of the USSR about the "Stalinist-Brezhnevist" composition of the commission was not ungrounded.

---

[61]*Izvestia*, 25 December 1989.

The draft decision elaborated by the commission headed by Iacovlev received fewer votes (1027) than necessary (1122) for its adoption as a decision of the Congress. Realizing that this vote threatened to expose the "new political thinking" in front of the whole world, Gorbachev and Luchianov did their best so that the draft decision would be discussed again on the next day at the meeting of the Congress. One of the deputies, namely M. Munteanu from Soviet Moldavia, declared during the debates: "With respect to the nonexistence of these treaties, I want to say that the whole world considers that they exist, but we do not admit" this fact.[62]

The main "argument" set forth by the deputies who voted against the draft decision of the commission was that its adoption would mean that "the Congress blames nonexistent documents" (deputy A. Irgaşev) and that the USSR and its people were directly accused "of unleashing World War II" (deputy V. Klokov).

And so, overnight, incontestable evidence appeared that the originals of the additional secret protocol existed in the Soviet archives at least until 1946. Thus, the next day (24 December 1989) A. Iacovlev read the text of the following document dated April 1946, which is preserved in the archives of the Ministry of Foreign Affairs of the USSR:

"We, the undersigned, Smirnov, deputy head of comrade Molotov's Secretariate, and Podțerob, superior assistant of the Minister of Foreign Affairs, on this date the former turned over to the latter the following documents from the special archives of the Ministry of Foreign Affairs of the USSR:

1. The original copy of the additional secret protocol of 23 August 1939 in Russian and German, plus three copies of this protocol."[63]

In addition, Iacovlev related that "the protocols, after which the West German photocopies were made, had been typed with the same

---

[62]Ibid.

[63]Ibid.

typewriter used for the original copy of the treaty which is preserved in the archives of the Ministry of Foreign Affairs of the USSR."[64]

After he presented the incontestable evidence that the additional secret protocol existed, Iacovlev tried to attenuate here and there the formulations of the draft decision which had been discussed by the deputies the day before, but without changing anything of its essence. Thus, for instance, in the attenuated text, the fragment of the draft decision in which the term *the authenticity* of the additional secret protocol was used was given the following form: "the graphological, photo-technical, and lexical examinations of the copies, maps, and other documents, and the concordance of the subsequent events with the contents of the protocol confirm the fact of its signing and of its existence."[65]

Despite the fact that indisputable evidence proved the existence of the protocol and the formal modifications of the draft decision, 252 deputies voted against it and 264 abstained from voting. It was, nevertheless, adopted with 1432 votes as decision of the Congress.

Trying to do their best to convince the deputies to vote for the draft decision of the commission, Gorbachev and his men were finally forced to admit the historical truth.

In all the material we mentioned above, beginning with the report presented in the name of the commission and ending with the decision adopted by the Congress, there is a strict delimitation between the Soviet-German Treaty itself and the additional secret protocol in the sense that, as Iacovlev maintained at the meeting of 24 December 1989, the first was a "legal, justified" (*pravomernyi, obosnovannyi*) act, while the second must be considered as "unacceptable, morally inappropriate, incompatible with Socialism" (*moral'no negodnyi, nepriemlemyi, neosovmestimyi s sotsializmom*). Iacovlev's affirmation that the Soviet-German Treaty itself was a "legal and justified" act can only mean one thing, namely that the Gorbachevist leadership of the USSR was trying to mislead the public. The assertion that "Stalin and his entourage" and not "the pre-War Soviet leadership" were the only ones responsible for the

---

[64]Ibid.

[65]Ibid.

invading essence of the Molotov-Ribbentrop Pact was made with the same purpose.

In the same report presented by Iacovlev it is said on the one hand, in full concordance with the historical truth, that "choosing the way of sharing the booty with the plunderer, Stalin began to use the language of ultimatums and threats toward neighboring countries, especially small countries," and on the other hand, in flagrant contradiction with the historical truth, it is claimed that Stalin thus obtained "the return of Bessarabia within the composition of the Soviet Union, the reestablishment of Soviet power in the Baltic republics."[66] Despite Iacovlev's categorical criticism of the imperialist means to which Stalin resorted to obtain the so-called "return" of Bessarabia and the so-called "reestablishment" of Soviet power in the Baltic States, it is a fact that he himself considered as totally valid and well-grounded the terminology elaborated on the basis of the Stalinist slogans. Considering this eclecticism, which was a consequence of the double-dealing policy of the Gorbachevist leadership of the USSR, it is not surprising that deputy L. Iorga (Leonida Lari) put Iacovlev in a difficult situation with her question-reply: "As Bessarabia was a colony of the Tsarist Empire, why did you say that it was returned, as if it was a property of the Soviet Union, of Russia? And, as only Bessarabia was indicated in the pact, why did Stalin occupy also Moldavia and Bucovina, instead of annexing only Bessarabia? As a matter of fact, Bessarabia includes only the regions of Akkerman, Chilia, and Ismail which are now in the Ukraine."

The courageous question-reply of Leonida Lari was totally ignored by Iacovlev and was not reflected in the decision of the Congress of Deputies of the People of the USSR. In return, however, the essence of this question-reply was seriously taken into consideration by the commission created by the parliament of the Republic of Moldavia, whose report was approved on 23 June 1990 by the decision of the Supreme Soviet of the SSR of Moldavia. In total contradiction with the formulations of the decision of the second Congress of People's Deputies of the USSR, adopted on the basis of

---

[66]Ibid.

the draft decision of the commission headed by Iacovlev, and in absolute concordance with the historical truth, the report of the respective commission from the SSR of Moldavia is based on the following conclusions:

1) "Bessarabia and Northern Bucovina were always integral parts of the State of Moldavia, created in the fourteenth century on the territory of the Romanians's ancestors — the Geto-Dacians."

2) "In 1812 Russia dismembered the State of Moldavia, annexing the territory between the Prut and the Dniester Rivers, artificially extending over it the name of *Bessarabia*."

3) "On 27 March 1918... the *Sfatul Țării* voted for the unification of Bessarabia with Romania. On 15 November 1918 the General Congress of Bucovina voted for "The unconditional and permanent unification of Bucovina with the Romanian Kingdom..."

4) "The insistent affirmations of official Soviet historiography that the Soviet power established in Bessarabia in 1918 and that the latter became this way an integral part of the Soviet State had the purpose of motivating the export of the revolution, seeking a new annexation of Bessarabia."

5) "The notes with the nature of an ultimatum of 26 and 27 June 1940 contravene the fundamental standards of international law and are examples of the policy of imperial dictate. The decision regarding the occupation of Northern Bucovina represents an eloquent example of the expansionist policy that was permanently promoted by the Stalinist government. On 28 June 1940 the USSR occupied by military force Bessarabia and Northern Bucovina, contrary to the wishes of the population of those regions. The illegal proclamation, on 2 August 1940, of the SSR of Moldavia was an act of dismemberment of Bessarabia and Bucovina. The arbitrary placing of Northern Bucovina and the counties Hotin, Ismail, and Cetatea Albă under the jurisdiction of the SSR of the Ukraine was in contradiction with the historical truth and the real ethnic situation of that time."[67]

These quotes prove that the parliament of the SSR of Moldavia disapproved not only of the additional secret protocol, but, unlike the commission headed by Iacovlev and the Congress of People's

---

[67] *Sovetskaia Moldavia*, 28 June 1990.

Deputies, also of the Soviet-German Pact of 23 August 1939 and especially its consequences.

In conclusion, the following facts should be emphasized:

1. In the year 1812, when the Tsarist Empire occupied the territory between the Prut and the Dniester Rivers belonging to the principality of Moldavia, the Russians made the first step toward what later became "the problem of Bessarabia," by extending "the name of Bessarabia, which originally designated only the eastern part, by the Danube, once ruled over by the Wallachian Basarabs, over the whole region between the Prut and the Dniester."

2. After the defeat suffered in the Crimean War, Russia, in conformity with the Peace Treaty of Paris (1856), using the stratagem of 1812, ceded *under the name of Bessarabia* only the southern counties of the territory seized by the dismemberment of the Principality of Moldavia.

3. On 28 June 1940 the Soviet Empire reannexed Bessarabia and, in addition, annexed Northern Bucovina and thus dismembered the Romanian kingdom.

4. Through the law of 2 August 1940 Moscow dismembered and at the same time dissolved the autonomous Moldavian republic that it had created in 1924 on the territory of the Ukraine with a view to the reannexation, at an opportune moment, of Bessarabia.

5. By the same law Bessarabia was dismembered, its southern part (the counties of Cetatea Albă and Ismail) and its northern part (Hotin county) were incorporated into the Ukraine.

Irreconcilable Internal Conflicts: "Pro-USSR Romanians" and "Pro-Romania Romanians"

The political-administrative and territorial changes made in a totally arbitrary manner by Moscow through the law of 2 August 1940 — the formation of the *Union* Moldavian Republic (through the dismemberment of Bessarabia and the dissolution of the *autonomous* Moldavian republic on the left side of the Dniester), the inclusion of the counties of Cetatea Albă and Ismail in southern Bessarabia, and of the Hotin county in the north within the Ukraine, the incorporation of Northern Bucovina and of the Herța district into the Ukraine — all these were included in the substratum of Leonida Lari's question-reply that she expressed at the second Congress of People's Deputies of the USSR in December 1989. And the long-lasting consequences of these arbitrary changes could be noticed in the political life of the republic, especially in the dissensions existing among the representatives of the native population in regard to the position that was to be taken concerning the topical problems.

One of these radical problems, one could say the key problem from the point of view of the future of the republic's population, is undoubtedly that of an eventual unification with Romania. The fact that this problem was brought up even by the Communist Party of Soviet Moldavia both by decisions adopted directly at its sessions, as well as by "sociological investigations" organized by scientific institutions subordinated to it, shows that the problem became so acute that it could not be passed over in silence any longer. The *identity* between the *position* of the Central Committee, reflected in the decision of its plenary session of March 1990, and the *subsequent conclusions* of such an investigation finds its expression in the transplantation of certain formulas from the "decision" of the plenary session into the "conclusions" of the scientists who conducted the investigation. For example: The Decision of the Plenary Session of the Central Committee:

"The Communist Party of Moldavia records that the peoples that have been living for centuries and were formed on their national territories within the present frontiers of the two neighboring sovereign states, Romania and the SSR of Moldavia, who have a common language, culture, and origin, will continue their relations on the basis of the steadfast observance of the Helsinki Agreement regarding the inviolability of borders in Europe.[68]

The scientists's conclusions:

"The investigations demonstrated that 60% of those who were questioned are of the opinion that the peoples who formed on their own national territories within the present borders of the two neighboring sovereign states, Romania and the SSR of Moldavia, who have a common language, culture, and origin, have to build their

---

[68]*Moldova Socialistă*, 4 April 1990.

relations on the basis of a strict observance of the Helsinki Agreement regarding the stability of frontiers in Europe."[69]

The previous fragments were reproduced in the article "Ce sîntem și ce vrem?" ("What are we and what do we want?"), published by Emil Mândâcanu in the weekly *Literatura și Arta*. Analyzing the "conclusions" drawn by G. Entelis and A. Timuș, and showing how tendentious are not only these "conclusions," but also the questions that were elaborated for the "sociological investigation," E. Mândâcanu asks, with good reason: "How can Petru Lucinschi, the first secretary of the Central Committee of the Moldavian Communist Party, after reading the results of this investigation performed by an institution subordinated precisely to the respective Central Committee, conclude the following: "The comments... are useless" and thus "the case is closed."[70]

Mândâcanu compared the two fragments to point out that it is not a matter of a mere fortuitous coincidence. And we have to take into consideration that the texts were not reproduced after their originals (Entelis and Timuș wrote their works in Russian, and the Central Committee used the same language to elaborate its materials), but after their translations, as they appeared in *Moldova Socialistă*. We suppose that the resemblance of the two texts would be even more striking if they were compared in the language they were written in. But nevertheless it is still clear that the author of the text which presents the conclusions of the "sociological investigation" is the same person who prepared the material for the "decision" of the Central Committee.

Mândâcanu's article is important not only because it deals with the inveterate *Mankurts* from the Central Committee of the Moldavian Communist Party and from the scientific institutions of the republic, who do their best to promote in a new, disguised form the old policy of subordinating the national vital interests of the republic's native population to Moscow's imperial interests. Besides giving a riposte to the *Mankurts*, Mândâcanu concentrated his attention especially on the native population and the divergences

---

[69] Ibid. 17 July 1990.

[70] E. Mândâcanu, "Ce sîntem și ce vrem?" in *Literatura și Arta*, 9 August 1990.

which exist among different groups of the population regarding the position that should be taken to secure the future of the latter as a national-ethnic entity.

The author of the article "Ce sîntem și ce vrem?" considers that after the second Congress of the Popular Front of Moldavia the emphasis of the discussions among the natives moved from the alternative of remaining within the USSR or not, to the alternative of uniting with Romania or not. He concludes, in broad outline, that "the native population is divided into four groups with four distinct opinions: 1. we are Moldavians (a separate people) and we want to be part of the USSR; 2. we are Moldavians (a separate people), but we want our republic to become an independent state; 3. we are Romanians (Moldavian Romanians), but we want to live as an independent state; 4. we are Romanians (Moldavian Romanians) and we want to unite with Romania."[71]

In correlation to this classification, the author names, conventionally, the first group "the pro-USSR Moldavians," the second group "the pro-independence Moldavians," the third group "the pro-independence Romanians," and the fourth group "the pro-Romania Romanians." At the same time Mândâcanu points out that the part of the natives ("a number of denationalized intellectuals" and " good number of peasants and workers with a low intellectual level") that belong to the first group are easily manipulated by the representatives of the ruling administrative system. On the other hand, stressing on the divergences between the second, the third, and the fourth groups, E. Mândâcanu mentions that "one could presume that at a certain moment of more intense polarization an important part of 'the pro-independence Moldavians' could transfer to the group of 'the pro-independence Romanians' or even of 'the pro-Romania Romanians.'"[72]

After surveying the four groups, the author of the article expressed his opinion that, in the present period of great unrest, "it is normal to exist different views regarding the future of this long-suffering piece of land," but "the intrigue among certain leaders or

---

[71]Ibid.

[72]Ibid.

representatives of different trends is not normal." He goes on saying that through their reciprocal attacks the leaders of these groups "do a disservice to the cause, mislead the masses, and disunite the movement of national liberation from within, instead of trying to reach the necessary consensus to give the proper riposte to the forces that oppose this movement and undermine it from the outside."

One could say that only the leaders and the inspirers of the fourth group — of "the pro-Romania Romanians" — are consistent in their position toward the key problems regarding the future of the natives as an integral part of the Romanian people. And it is not surprising that the writers Grigore Vieru, Leonida Lari, Dumitru Matcovschi, Nicolae Dabija, Vladimir Beşleagă, and other spiritual leaders of the "pro-Romania Romanians" are the ones attacked by the Russophones and the *Mankurts*. The persons who can be considered as representatives of the other three groups are all inconsistent and without well-defined principles, thus differing among each other, not only according to the groups in which they should be included, but also within the same group. For example, V. Iovv, A. Lazarev, Petru Lucinschi, A. Lupan, V. Senic, V. Stati, K. Stratievschi, V. Taranov, and many others should be considered (according to their passports) "pro-USSR Moldavians." There is, of course, a great difference between, let us say, the position and the views of the poet Andrei Lupan and those of Vasile Iovv, the former party leader for the city of Bălţi, about whom 124 inhabitants of the locality wrote that "he should be held responsible... for the crimes committed in this city" and that "at the historic session of the Supreme Soviet of the SSR of Moldavia he was against the proclamation of the state language and the adoption of the Latin alphabet."[73] Andrei Lupan's "merits" differ from those of his fellow member of the group of "pro-USSR Moldavians" and colleagues within the Bureau of the Central Committee, in the sense that he can not be accused of the abuses and crimes attributed to Iovv. At the 17th Congress of the Organization of the Communist Party of the Republic, Andrei Lupan declared, among other things, that in the past the Moldavian writers would come to the towns on the left side of the Dniester where they were

---

[73]*Literatura şi Arta*, 21 June 1990.

welcomed "with bread and salt" by the workers, the students, and the intellectuals, and that "although today that period is being characterized with epithets like 'Stalinism' and 'Brezhnevism,' it is then that the sacred and durable sentiments were implanted." Further on he addressed the delegates with the following words: "I appeal to you, communist comrades, let us try to revive all these, to organize again such meetings in the schools of the towns on the left side of the Dniester, to educate the children in the spirit of friendship and mutual respect."[74]

We can thus see that Lupan was dreaming of the "revival" of *the golden era*, in his opinion, of Stalin and Brezhnev. It is under Stalin that he became president of the Leading Committee of the Writers's Union of Moldavia, and then, under Stalin's successors, secretary of the Writers's Union of the USSR. Under Khrushchev, in 1961, Ioan Bodiul made him and none of the other writers a member of the Academy of Sciences of the Republic. After Bodiul's removal and the naming of Semion Grossu in the position of first secretary of the party, Lupan was one of the first to be conferred with the honorific title of writer of the people, and under Lucinschi he became a member of the Bureau of the Central Committee. Thus, it is not surprising that he was in the group of "pro-USSR Moldavians."

It is true that Andrei Lupan was a member of the Bessarabian underground communist organization before the events of the year 1940. But it is also true that, although before these events he criticized Bessarabian realities in his writings, he did not declare himself in favor of the "reestablishment" of Soviet power or, at least, of its establishment in Bessarabia.

As we have already mentioned, there is a great difference between "the pro-USSR Moldavians" of Lupan's kind on the one hand, and of Iovv's kind on the other hand. This is because, first of all, men like Iovv could be held responsible for criminal acts.

With regard to Andrei Lupan, we could add the following: during the period between the years 1918 and 1940, the Bessarabian underground communist movement was inspired and controlled by agents systematically infiltrated by Moscow on the territory of the

---

[74] *Sovetskaia Moldavia*, 29 May 1990.

Romanian state. A large number of the participants in this movement joined it being misled by its socio-economic objectives, as they were formulated in the proclamations and the slogans of the communist underground. In the years 1930s the communist movement attracted Andrei Lupan as well who, we have to suppose (there is no reason not to suppose), believed that the socio-economic claims of the communists derived from the most sincere and noble intentions. And he repeatedly adopted an attitude critical of the Romanian, and especially the Bessarabian, situation, which during that period were indeed, in many ways, as bleak as possible. Thus, one could say that in that period Lupan was a nonconformist, a revolutionary, in the sense that he opposed the regime existing in Romania at that time. However, after the events of the year 1940 until the last period of his life he *systematically* acted as an irremediable conformist, reconciled with the ways of the Soviet regime.

Another "pro-USSR Moldavian," also an octogenarian, who continues to obstinately maintain the theses and slogans of the past, is the historian A. Lazarev, the author of the famous monograph *Moldavskaia sovetskaia gosudarstvennost' i bessarabskii vopros* (1974), which brought him all sorts of titles in the republic. In the years when Brezhnev was the leader of the communist organization of the republic Lazarev was named secretary of the Central Committee and member of the Bureau of the Central Committee. As a political figure, A. Lazarev distinguished himself through his attacks against the Bessarabian writers (Liviu Deleanu, Iosif Balţan, etc.) during the famous campaign against cosmopolitanism. After Brezhnev left the republic the political career of Lazarev began to decline; he first lost his position of secretary of the Central Committee, being named Minister of Culture, subsequently being dismissed from this position as well. As already in 1950 he had published a brochure entitled *Formarea RSS Moldoveneşti* (*The Formation of the SSR of Moldavia*). When he decided to dedicate himself to the scientific work he chose as a principal subject of study the history of Moldavia and especially the problem of Bessarabia. In his scientific career he ascended as rapidly as in his political one; he was first a candidate and then a Doctor of Sciences, a corresponding member and then an active member of the Academy of Sciences and also its vice-president, the rector of the University of Chişinău, etc.

All these were a result of his being the most impetuous and the most aggressive preacher of Moscow's interests regarding the problem of Bessarabia.

We mentioned earlier what kind of role Lazarev had at the "round tables" of Lucinschi and how he played it. But the Supreme Soviet approved the conclusions of the commission created for the political and juridical evaluation of the Soviet-German Pact of August 1939 and of the additional secret protocol. Only three days after the publication of the conclusions of the commission and of the respective decision of the parliament of the republic, the newspaper *Sovetskaia Moldavia* reserved *a whole page* for an article written by Lazarev. The size of the article and the date of its publication indicate that it had been prepared beforehand at the order of the Central Committee, possibly of the first secretary himself, to counteract the predictable conclusions of the commission of the republic's parliament.

Another indication in this sense, on the one hand, is that in this article Lazarev vehemently criticized a) those "adult children who deny their parents who gave them life, their mother tongue which served as a connecting bridge between parents and their children, their own name given to them by their parents," and b) "some of the representatives of the Moldavian nation" who "try to destroy the real existence of their parents, namely the Moldavian people itself, when they try to prove the absence of the real and durable means of their contact with their own parents, namely the Moldavian language itself, when they recklessly disavow the name which their ancestors had for centuries, that is the name Moldavian."[75] On the other hand, when he talked about the past of the region and criticized non-Soviet authors, especially Romanian historians on the right side of the Prut, he resorted to obsolete theses and formulas and to the compromised terminology which he had used in his principal work of 1974.

Only some elements of a single affirmation made by Lazarev in this article could be accepted, with certain fundamental objections not only by "the pro-independence Romanians" (the third group), but also by "the pro-Romania Romanians) (the fourth group). This affirmation is that "the process of its complete and definitive consolidation (of the

---

[75] A. Lazarev, "Ia moldovanin!" in *Sovetskaia Moldavia*, 26 June 1990.

Moldavian bourgeois nation) took place within eastern Moldavia, that is *on the territory of the whole Bessarabia and of Moldavia on the left side of the Dniester* which with the completion of the process of the nation's formation began to be called national Moldavian territory, and only the nation that formed on this territory acquired the right to rule over it and possess it."

The words written in italics could seem too daring for "the pro-USSR Moldavians" and even for "the pro-independence Moldavians" because in their essence they are a reprobation not only of the dismemberment of Bessarabia by the law adopted by the Supreme Soviet on 2 August 1940, but also of the actual disintegration of Moldavia on the left side of the Dniester, namely of both territories which, in conformity with the theory of the author, *the nation that formed on them could exclusively possess*.

The subtleties of this position of the author must be sought, on the one hand, in the appearance in 1924, on the left bank of the Dniester, and the disappearance in 1940 of that political-administrative organization which was called the Autonomous Soviet Socialist Republic of Moldavia, and, on the other hand, in the dismemberment in 1940 of Bessarabia, which in Soviet documents and in the documents of the Bessarabian communist underground was considered, *in its whole*, as an integral part of the USSR (of the Ukraine) during the period 1918-1924, and, subsequently, of the Autonomous Soviet Socialist Republic of Moldavia during the years 1924-1940.

This position is anchored with its implications in the acute political problems and inter-ethnic relations of our times, that is in the realities of the republic from the beginning of the last decade of the twentieth century, in the sense that it attacked both the Russophones from Tiraspol who try to take away from the republic the districts on the left side of the Dniester and to form an Autonomous Nistrian Republic (in which Tighina and its surroundings would also be included), as well as the leaders of the "Gagauz halcî" movement, which proclaimed an Autonomous Gagauz Republic in Comrat and its surroundings, removed from the jurisdiction of the SSR of Moldavia and directly subordinate to Moscow. Precisely and exclusively from this point of view the "pro-independence

Romanians" and even "the pro-Romania Romanians" could share Lazarev's position.

With the exception of the elements mentioned above which could be acceptable, to a certain extent, to the "pro-independence Romanians" and "the pro-Romania Romanians," the rest of the article and even of the affirmation in which Lazarev included those elements is in flagrant disagreement with the historical truth, as well as with the aspirations of the Romanians from both groups, and also with the most elementary standards of scientific ethics. Thus, he uses in a totally artificial manner the term *Eastern Moldavia* (*Vostochnaia Moldavai*) as a synonym of the whole of Bessarabia along with the whole territory of the former autonomous Republic of Moldavia which was created in 1924. Not less artificial is the usage in the given context of the term *Moldavia on the left bank of the Dniester* (*Levoberezhnaia Moldavia*) as a synonym of the whole territory of the former Autonomous Republic. The affirmation that on the mentioned territories a process of complete and definitive consolidation of the *Moldavian bourgeois nation* took place represents a "contribution" to the Soviet historiography with a thesis totally in agreement with the usage of the term *Eastern Moldavia* for designating certain territories which never existed in reality as a unified administrative and cultural entity. But this thesis does not find its confirmation in the processes and phenomena of the epoch which Lazarev refers to. On the contrary, these processes and phenomena prove that *only on the territory of Bessarabia*, although the province had been annexed in 1812 by the Russian Empire, a long process of strengthening the cultural and spiritual ties with the other Romanian territories took place, which finally contributed to the completion and consolidation of the *Romanian nation*, and not of a Moldavian nation different from the Romanian one.

Patriotic Nationalism and Chauvinistic Nationalism

A riposte given by Ion Țurcanu to A. Lazarev could serve for a better understanding of the essence of the harsh controversies regarding the past, the present, and the future of the natives in view of the four groups into which E. Mândâcanu conventionally divides them. The fact that this riposte appeared in the same newspaper which a few days earlier had published Lazarev's article is not surprising considering that its author then held the position of secretary of the Supreme Soviet of the republic.

Imputing the author of the article "Ia moldovanin!" ("I am a Moldavian!") that he labels all those who do not agree with him as "ignorants," "liars," and so on, in his riposte Ion Țurcanu resorts himself to such expressions as "the hatred toward the opponents," "the usage of lies," etc.

But it is not so much for the expressions which Ion Țurcanu resorts to in his totally justified accusation of Lazarev's position, as a certain detail of his riposte that shows that his position is not absolutely irreproachable either. Thus, for instance, Lazarev maintains that "the process of the formation of the Moldavian bourgeois nation attracted in the orbit of its consolidation also the Moldavians of Moldavia on the left side of the Dniester, as well as a certain part of other ethnic elements on both sides of the Dniester — the Ukrainians, the Russians, the Poles, the Gypsies, the Jews, the Bulgarians, and other ethnic elements that populated the area where the Moldavian nation formed."[76]

It is significant in this case that "the pro-Romania Romanian" Ion Țurcanu, although he vehemently and with good reason criticized "the pro-USSR Moldavian" Artiom Lazarev, at the same time resorts himself at the preferred methods of yesterday's historiography of Soviet Moldavia. Because what else could represent the way in which he reproduces Lazarev's thesis which was quoted earlier? Showing correctly that Lazarev maintained that in the second half of the nineteenth century a separate Moldavian nation formed east of the Prut, further on Țurcanu quoted him incorrectly: in Lazarev's opinion, "*the Ukrainians, the Russians, the Poles, the Gypsies, the Jews, the Bulgarians*, and other ethnic elements were attracted in this process."[77]

These words were translated from the respective riposte of Țurcanu. One could object that my translation is not correct, that

---

[76]A. Lazarev, op. cit., *Sovetskaia Moldavia*, 26 June 1990.

[77]Ion Țurcanu, "O natsional'noi gordosti moldavan kak ee ponimaet akademik Lazarev" in *Sovetskaia Moldavia*, 30 June 1990.

Ţurcanu meant to say that *Ukrainians, Russians, Poles*, etc. were attracted in this process, and not *the Ukrainians, the Russians, the Poles*. The absence in the Russian language of the grammatical category of the article (definite and indefinite) would justify at first sight such an objection, but only at first sight. Because if Ţurcanu meant "a certain part of other ethnic elements — of the Ukrainians, the Russians, the Poles" he would not have written a modified text between quotations marks presenting it as completely belonging to the quoted author. This modification was however necessary for Ţurcanu to draw the following conclusion: "I do not think that one could find another similar interpretation of the category of "nation" according to which the nation is constituted of the most various ethnic components."[78]

We have no reason to believe that Ţurcanu is not aware that there is no nation which formed out of a single ethnic component, that *certain Slavic ethnic elements* were assimilated by the more or less distant ancestors of the Romanians, that the Romanian nation assimilated many *Gypsies, Bulgarians*, and other ethnic elements. Precisely for this reason we have to consider that the explanation for his position is not at all his not knowing the facts, but rather his tendency to ignore these facts in order to appear in the eyes of the less initiated natives and of some intellectuals as a leader who truly fights for the salvation of the *purified* national being of the people.

In the eulogistic presentation which precedes the translation of the work *Russia, Romania and Bessarabia* (Chişinău, 1992, pp. 3-28), Ion Ţurcanu, considering as disputable my affirmation that "By the unification of the territory (in the context — of Bessarabia) with Romania, *the Moldavians, from their position of an oppressed nationality within the composition of Russia, became representatives of the dominant nation*" (p. 291), maintains the following: "Bruchis affirms that the Moldavians did not join in a body the Bessarabian communist movement, as they were allegedly part of the dominant nation, while those who participated in this movement 'were in their absolute majority representatives of the oppressed nations in Bessarabia.' We mention in short that in Bessarabia there never

---

[78]Ibid.

existed a mass communist movement in the inter-war period. What is more important though is the fact that the affirmations regarding the dominant nation and the oppressed nations do not really correspond with the Romanian realities between the two wars. Because the population of Bessarabia was made up mostly of Moldavian peasants, that is Romanians, but this large mass of people was living in very difficult conditions. On the other hand, a national minority, the Jews, for instance, were not part of the 'dominant nation' but despite this they led a comfortable life on account of that popular mass which formed the bulk of the 'dominant nation'." (Ion Țurcanu, "O carte instructivă și mult așteptată," preface to *Russia, Romania and Bessarabia*, p. 27).

This fragment was entirely reproduced here because it is a conspicuous reflection of the tendency even of a real Romanian patriot to deviate from certain incontestable facts when *it seems to him* that they could be interpreted in the disadvantage of the native population. However, the fact is, first of all, that:

1) By the unification in 1918 of Bessarabia with Romania the more than one hundred year *domination* of Tsarist Russia was ended and, during the inter-war period (1918-1940), the province was under *Romanian domination*. This is why the Romanian historian I. Nistor entitled one of his works *Basarabia sub dominațiunea românească (Bessarabia under Romanian domination)*, (Cernăuți, 1938);

2) "all the laws and reactionary measures adopted to the disadvantage of the national minorities in the Romanian Kingdom, such as, for example, 'the law for the protection of the national work,' 'numerus clausus,' 'numerus valachicus,' and others did not endanger the interests of the Bessarabian Moldavians, but, on the contrary, placed them in more advantageous conditions compared to other nationalities and created a privileged situation for them within the state."[79]

Secondly, Țurcanu's observation that "in Bessarabia there never existed a mass communist movement" gives the impression that this

---

[79] Michael Bruchis, *Rusia, România și Basarabia. 1812, 1918, 1924, 1940*. Translation from Russian by A. Chiriac. Kishinev, 1992, pp. 291, 257.

fact is not mentioned in the work *Russia, Romania and Bessarabia*. However, it is repeatedly emphasized in the book:

a) "the communists from Bessarabia did not represent a force of any importance" (p. 301);

b) "the communist organization of Bessarabia... counted a few hundreds of people (321 members in 1931, 279 members in 1934... In the last year of the period (1918-1940)... the Bessarabian underground counted 375 communists" (p. 300);

c) the percentage of Jewish participants in the communist movement from Bessarabia was by far greater than the percentage of the Jews within the whole population of the region" (p. 203).

Another totally unfounded affirmation made by Țurcanu is that the Jewish population of Bessarabia "led a comfortable life on the account of that popular mass which formed the bulk of the 'dominant nation.'" This assertion is in total agreement with the xenophobe attitude of *some* "pro-Romanian Romanians" who are *chauvinistic* nationalists and not *patriotic* nationalists in the true sense of the word. This affirmation is in accord with the spirit of those materials written by *some* chauvinistic nationalists (that lately appear even in some of the most imposing publications) which praise such historic figures as Corneliu Zelea Codreanu, Nichifor Crainic, and Ion Antonescu. And finally, this affirmation must be considered as a tribute paid by some patriotic nationalists to chauvinistic nationalists.

During the period 1918-1940 the number of the Jewish participants, although considerable among the underground communists from Bessarabia, was insignificant in relation to the number of the Jewish population of the province, as the number in general of the participants to the subversive communist movement from Bessarabia was insignificant when compared to the whole population of the region. At the same time, we can say that the number of the Jews who *were leading a comfortable life* in Bessarabia, and not only "on account of that popular mass which formed the bulk of the 'dominant population,'" as Țurcanu said, but also on account of the rest of the province's population, was insignificant in relation to the whole Jewish population. There were at that time some more or less wealthy Jewish elements (merchants, lawyers, doctors, owners of small workshops). But the majority of the Jewish population was made up of poor people who lived from one day to the next (tradesmen, workers, shopkeepers, and salesmen).

Viewed in historical perspective, the fourth group, that of "the pro-Romania Romanians," is the only one which expresses the vital interests of the Romanians east of the Prut as part of the Romanian people, a part which only within the borders of its reunified national state can be protected from an otherwise inevitable ethnic transformation and gradual alienation from the traditions, the language, and the culture of its people. With this purpose the leaders of "the pro-Romania Romanians" undertake a heroic struggle in the most difficult conditions, sometimes even at the risk of their own lives (Mircea Druc, I. Hadârcă, Grigore Vieru, Dumitru Matcovschi, Leonida Lari, etc.). However, as we mentioned earlier, also among "the pro-Romania Romanians" there are some who have prejudices regarding those of a different ethnic origin. One of these Romanians is Dinu Mihail, whose position, like Țurcanu's, cannot be considered as consistent. On the one hand Ion Țurcanu declares that "I do not want to doubt the right of existence of the SSR of Moldavia," and on the other hand he maintains: "but neither do we have the right to forget that the present Moldavian state was constituted in just a month, a very uncommon phenomenon even on the scale of world history."[80]

This *contraditio in adjecto* is not at all accidental. In the same article the author proclaims as a major task the entry of Moldavia in the Popular Front and the active participation "in this movement of as many *well-intentioned* people as possible, regardless of their nationality, party membership, religion, etc."[81] However, in an interview given before he became a deputy of the republic's parliament, the same Țurcanu rages against those who are *not of the same blood* with the Moldavian people, and ridicules those who talk of *well-intentioned people*, declaring that he is "very skeptical

---

[80] Ion Țurcanu, "August '39" in *Literatura și Arta*, 10 August 1989.

[81] Ibid.

regarding the creative potential, and even the good intentions of some of the well-intentioned people."[82]

The same thing can be said about the inherent contradictions of some materials signed by Dinu Mihail. Thus, he criticizes with good reason the school curriculum for Moldavian Literature requested for the "1990 Matriculation" in universities, the scientific orientation of those who elaborated it in the spirit of praising the influence of Russian literature and its classics, of the Soviet achievements and the role of the Communist Party in the development of the national literature. However, at the same time, Dinu Mihail introduces, between parentheses, a special remark in the following fragment: "The *Contemporanul* magazine and its fight (or rather *Solomon Kaţ's fight*) against the aesthetic REACTIONARY conceptions OF THE 'JUNIMEA' LITERARY SOCIETY."[83] (Both the italics as well as the capital letters are reproduced after Dinu Mihail's text).

It is anyone's indisputable right to share the fundamental principle of one of the two predominant trends of the national literature of that time, namely of "art for art's sake," whose theoretician was the spiritual father of the "Junimea" literary society, Titu Maiorescu, or of the "tendentious art," whose theoretician was the ideologist of the *Contemporanul* magazine, Solomon Kaţ. Very much of Ion Druţă's fiction and of Grigore Vieru's poems are not only impressive literary works, but also embodiments of the "tendentious art." Dinu Mihail, although everything he writes displays tendentiousness, has, of course, any right to declare himself in favor of the aesthetic orientation of "Junimea," and not that of *Contemporanul*. But it is a *sacrilege* to accuse *Solomon Kaţ* of fighting "against the aesthetic *reactionary* conceptions of the 'Junimea' literary society." And this is why:

a) In the article which he *considered as erroneous* and contradicted the aesthetic conceptions of the spiritual father of "Junimea," *Solomon Kaţ* did not use the epithet *reactionary* for characterizing these conceptions. The epithet belongs to the authors of the school curriculum for Moldavian literature, and not to *Solomon*

---

[82]*Literatura şi Arta*, 22 February 1990.

[83]Dinu Mihail, "The 1990 Matriculation" in *Literatura şi Arta*, 5 July 1990.

Kaţ who, while criticizing the erroneous conceptions, in his opinion, of Titu Maiorescu, talked at the same time with respect about his personality and did not insult him in any way. This cannot be said, unfortunately, about the means of expression to which Maiorescu resorted in a riposte addressed to Solomon Kaţ.[84]

b) I would estimate that the majority of Romanians both east and west of the Prut would not know who *Solomon Kaţ* was, but they would know who *Constantin Dobrogeanu-Gherea* was. There is no doubt that Dinu Mihail would rage against those who would write that Mihail *Eminovici* is the author of *Luceafărul*, and *Tadeu Hîjdeu* the author of the drama *Răzvan şi Vidra*, instead of calling them by the names they used for signing their works — Mihai Eminescu and Bogdan Petriceicu Hasdeu.

c) The poet Dimitrie Anghel, in his position of president of the Romanian Writers' Society, invited Dobrogeanu-Gherea to join this society. In his answer, published in *Adevărul* of 18 November 1909, Dobrogeanu-Gherea referred to the regulations of the Writers' Society which conditioned membership on the possession of the original copy of a birth certificate "signed by the mayor of the respective locality." Expressing his attitude in this matter, Dobrogeanu-Gherea remarked that as he "had the mischance to be born in Russia" he could not present the original copy of his birth certificate to prove that he "was really born."[85]

d) Dinu Mihail's observation that it was not *Contemporanul* itself, but "*rather Solomon Kaţ*" who fought against "Junimea" could be nothing else but an outspoken attack against *Solomon Kaţ not as an isolated Jew, but as an embodiment of all the Jews in general.*

When a representative of the dominant nation accuses the representatives of the national minorities or of a certain national minority of all the wrongdoings contaminating the country, thus giving rise to hatred against the latter, he cannot be considered as a nationalist in the true sense of the word. A real nationalist is one who defends the vital interests of his nation against those who attempt to

---

[84]Titu Maiorescu, *Critice*, vol. 2, Bucureşti, 1967, pp. 302-310.

[85]Constantin Dobrogeanu-Gherea, *Studii critice*, vol. 2, Bucureşti, 1956, pp. 401-403.

subdue it. But one who using the discontent of the popular masses caused by the situation within the country directs it against a national minority which suffers itself, sometimes even more than the native nation, from the same state of affairs, is not and cannot be considered a *nationalist*, because he is in fact a *chauvinist* who is looking for a scapegoat *at any price*.

Taken *as a whole*, as part of the Romanian people, the native population of Bessarabia was indeed exposed to a systematic process of denationalization that began in the year 1940 and continued at a rapid pace after the end of World War II. From this point of view the nationalism of the Romanians east of the Prut as a natural reaction to the imminent danger of their ethnic transformation and, finally, their Russification, was and continues to be a perfectly justified phenomenon. However, this does not mean that the representatives of the native population, taken as individuals, had more to suffer than, for instance, the Bessarabian Jews *taken as a whole*.

In its declaration of 13 May 1990, the Moldavian Popular Front characterized "all the inhuman and cruel acts, whose material, physical, and moral consequences are endured by the Jews, wherever they live, as concrete manifestations of anti-Semitism and condemns them."[86]

The truly patriotic national forces from the Republic of Moldavia are aware of the fact that anti-Semitism serves as an argument for the enemies of "the pro-Romania Romanians" and the "pro-independence Romanians" and this is why they published the "Declaration" of 13 May 1990 in which they emphasized that "the Moldavian Popular Front considers as categorically incompatible with its activities collaboration with persons, organizations, movements, parties, etc., with an outspoken or disguised anti-Jewish, anti-national orientation in general."[87]

---

[86]*Literatura şi Arta*, 24 May 1990.

[87]Ibid., 24 May 1990.

IV. GORBACHEV AS A PROMOTER OF SOVIET IMPERIALISM

"Friends from Moldavia" and "Deputies at all Levels"

As in other non-Russian republics of the former USSR, many representatives of the national minorities, as well as representatives of the native population have been members of the camp of the so-called internationalists known in Moldavia as "*Edinstvo*" (Unity). It is not a paradox that this camp-movement is inspired and guided by representatives of the Russian population and it is not surprising that most of the "pro-USSR Moldavians" are among its members. What is a paradox is that significant strata of the non-Romanian and non-Russian or non-Ukrainian population of Bessarabia, which have had to suffer even more than the natives from the national policy promoted by Moscow in the republic, are inspired by the internationalists or are members of their camp and not of the Moldavian Popular Front. And this despite the fact that, for instance, the whole Gagauz population and a significant part of the Jews of the republic have deep roots in Bessarabia, and that in 1940 Moscow divided in a totally arbitrary way the Bessarabian Gagauz population, including part of it in Moldavia and part in the Ukraine, and during the following years promoted a policy of Russification of the Gagauz at an even more rapid pace than in the case of the Moldavians.

Extending the essence of the conventional term "pro-USSR Moldavians" over the whole period of Soviet rule in the SSR of Moldavia, we notice that both the foreigners Borodin, Brezhnev, Serdiuc, as well as "the pro-USSR Moldavians" Salagor, Coval, Gladchi, Bodiul, Grossu, and Lucinschi, who succeeded each other in power, promoted Moscow's national policy in the republic to the disadvantage of the vital interests not only of the native population, but also of the national minorities, including the Gagauz. And from this point of view it is not as much the native population as Moscow and its imperialist policy that should be blamed.

The Gagauz intellectuals, who initiated the "Gagauz halcî" movement and instigated the proclamation of the Autonomous Gagauz Republic as part of the USSR, independent from Moldavia, are not in fact fighters for the good of their conationals, but rather careerists trying to gain some privileges within the Soviet system. Relevant evidence in this respect is that Russian was declared the state language in the so-called Autonomous Republic, instead of the Gagauz language. And this fact is an indication of the influence exerted by the internationalists on the actions of the Gagauz leaders.

When the parliament of the Republic of Moldavia began to legislate measures that were paving the way for the transformation of the republic into an independent and sovereign state, Moscow, in order to restrain the "recalcitrant" natives, did not stop but rather encouraged the actions that finally led to the attempt of the Russophones from Tiraspol-Tighina and that of the leaders of the "Gagauz halcî" movement to dismember Moldavia through the proclamation of a Nistrian Republic with its capital in Tiraspol, and of a Gagauz Republic, with its capital in Comrat. Moscow stimulated these attempts, considering that the natives, intimidated and frightened, would renounce their national aspirations.

From the very beginning, Gorbachev and his men never had any intention of allowing these attempts to become reality, that is they did not plan to proceed to a new dismemberment of the territory of the natives as they knew that such an action could have the effect of a chain reaction and that it was not in their best interest to bring the tanks in action once again and to resort to bloodshed in Moldavia as well.

This is why at the point when, from Moscow's point of view, the limit reached by the Russophones and the *Mankurts* on the left side of the Dniester could not be passed, from high quarters came the order: "as you were!" It is only at this moment that the president of the USSR appeared on the scene in the role of a mediator who assumed the mission of doing justice. First of all, as Mircea Snegur pointed out in an interview presented by the central television on 4 September 1990, Gorbachev assured him that he would support maintenance of the territorial integrity of the republic. Secondly, on 12 September 1990, Gorbachev met with "Soviet deputies from parts of the SSR of Moldavia" in the Kremlin during which, as the TASS agency reported, the participants expressed opinions that a)"the situation of inter-ethnic relations within the republic had become very tense and that urgent measures are required;" b)"the causes of this tension result from the mistakes made by the leadership of the republic in the national policy, from the ambiguity of some documents which were adopted, and of the position toward the Union (toward the USSR);" c) the problems that appeared must be resolved by observing the Constitution, by trying to find a solution reciprocally acceptable."[88]

And, more than that, according to the Soviet press agency, "the deputies (of the Republic of Moldavia) asked the president (Gorbachev) to send to the republic a commission of the Supreme Soviet of the USSR and of the Presidential Council to help find a conciliatory solution to the problems."[89]

These types of official news releases were not edited by the staff of the TASS agency, but by the closest counsellors of the president of the USSR. The predominant tone which crossed the whole text like a red thread was hypocrisy, because what else could denote, for example, the declaration that the problems of the republic which considers itself sovereign and is proclaimed sovereign by the Constitution of the USSR "must be resolved by observing the Constitution (of the USSR)? And what else could indicate the affirmation that "the causes of the tension" between the natives and

---

[88]*Pravda*, 13 September 1990.

[89]Ibid.

the non-natives in the SSR of Moldavia "result from the mistakes made by the leadership of the republic in the national policy," when in fact the Russophones and the *Mankurts*, protected by Moscow, and the Gagauz leaders instigated by them, are the ones who during the last years have carried on a systematic campaign of sabotaging the decisions of the parliament of the republic regarding the national language of the native population and the adoption of the Latin alphabet, the national symbols, and the gradual transformation of the SSR of Moldavia in a truly sovereign state?

Another indication of hypocrisy is the assertion that "the deputies (*deputaty*) asked Gorbachev *to send to the republic a commission of the Supreme Soviet of the USSR and of the Presidential Council."* And this is why:

a) The Russian language does not have the grammatical category of the article (definite - indefinite). Despite this there is no doubt that in the first lines of the information presented by the Soviet press agency the words *"vstrech Prezidenta SSSR s narodnmyi deputatami SSSR ot SSR Moldova"* mean that Gorbachev had a meeting with *deputies* (with some deputies, with a few deputies, with a group of deputies) of the USSR on the part of Moldavia, and not with *the deputies* (with all the deputies) of the republic;

b) it is the context that indicates in the Russian language whether the noun is individualized or known by the reader (listener). But if we take the microcontext, in our case the whole information, we notice that, *formally*, it is not sufficient to conclude that the noun *deputaty* does not mean *the deputies*, but *deputies*, in other words that *not all the deputies on the part of the SSR of Moldavia participated in the meeting with Gorbachev*. On the other hand, the macrocontext, among other things the available information regarding *the Soviet deputies on the part of Moldavia*, which can be found in official Soviet sources, clearly show that in this case the word *deputaty* means *some deputies, and not all the USSR deputies on the part of Moldavia.*

Thus, on the one hand, the information of the TASS agency does not specify the names of *the Soviet deputies on the part of Moldavia*, and on the other hand we do not have specific information on who exactly those persons were who, as the official news purposely suggests, *represented the will of the whole population of the republic*.

A PROMOTER OF SOVIET IMPERIALISM 143

But considering the *national and political position* of the various Soviet deputies on the part of Moldavia *we are able to say with certainty from among which deputies* were chosen the ones who participated in the meeting with Gorbachev.

We can say for certain that Dumitru Matcovschi, Ion Hadîrcă, Grigore Vieru, Nicolae Dabija, Anton Grăjdieru, and Leonida Lari did not take part in the meeting with Gorbachev, or, in case that some of these USSR deputies on the part of Moldavia did participate in that meeting, they were not the ones who asked Gorbachev to send to the republic a commission of the Supreme Soviet of the USSR and of the Presidential Council.

Through her entire political activity and poetical creation Leonida Lari proved that she is a member of the "pro-Romania Romanians" group, and that even if she participated in the meeting with Gorbachev along with other Soviet deputies on the part of Moldavia who "really want to protect the rights of the people," they were not in majority but in minority among the deputies on the part of the republic and that, in any case, they did not ask Gorbachev to send a commission to the republic.

On the other hand, we can be certain that some of the following Soviet deputies on the part of the SSR of Moldavia like, for example, Serghei Feodorovici Ahromeev, Simion Cuzmici Grossu, Alexandru Alexandrovici Mocanu, Iurii Vasilievici Blohin, Timotei Vasilievici Moşneaga, and Nelea Pavlovna Chiriac took part in the respective meeting, and that precisely to this category belonged the deputies who asked Gorbachev to send a commission to the republic. Leonida Lari, who had the courage to tell Gorbachev directly that "the parliament (of the USSR) is constituted on illegal basis" and to declare to the leaders of the Council of the National Salvation Front that it was necessary "to bring up the question of Bessarabia,"[90] could not have possibly asked Gorbachev to send the commission. He could have been asked only by such deputies as Timotei Moşneaga who, taking the floor during the debates of the first Congress of People's Deputies of the USSR and talking about the resistance to Moscow by some deputies, exclaimed: "You want to provoke the resistance of

---

[90] *Literatura şi Arta*, 15 February 1990.

both the union and the autonomous republics at the same time. Is this a just an intention? Will it awaken esteem for Moscow — the capital of our Soviet fatherland?"[91] Or by the "pro-USSR Moldavian" Nelea Chiriac who, at the same session of the Congress, praised the Communist Party and its General Secretary, declaring that "our party is the initiator of the reorganization. More exactly, its initiator is Mihail Sergheevici Gorbachev," to whom the deputies "practically and unanimously entrusted... the fate of the country..."[92]

Among those whom Mircea Snegur, in the report presented on 2 September 1990 at the second extraordinary session of the Supreme Soviet of Moldavia, accused of being "the initiators, organizers, and leaders of the recent illegal actions,"[93] Iurii Blohin is also mentioned. During the second Congress of People's Deputies of the USSR Iurii Blohin, a Soviet deputy on the part of the SSR of Moldavia, accused the Parliament of Moldavia that the laws it had adopted "when resolving the problem of sovereignty have a discriminating character," and he affirmed with hypocrisy that "a comrade from a Baltic republic mentioned that the rights of the national minorities must be protected. In the SSR of Moldavia I am also a national minority."[94] As they are part of the dominant nation of the USSR, those like Blohin cannot accept those laws of the Moldavian Parliament which represent the first steps toward the raising of the natives to the rank they deserve on their own land. And they try not only to undermine the transformation of Moldavia into a sovereign state, but also to provoke the hatred of the non-natives against the native population, instigating them to proclaim independent autonomies on the territory of the republic.

Moscow provoked and stimulated the actions of those like Iurii Blohin, V. Iacovlev, A. Lisetsky, V. Stati. V. Grosul, A. Borş, V. Iovv, and many others which finally led to the destabilization of interethnic relations within the republic. However, even when the

---

[91] *Izvestia*, 29 May 1989.

[92] Ibid.

[93] *Literatura şi Arta*, 29 June 1989.

[94] *Izvestia*, 14 December 1989.

dissensions went beyond the interests of Moscow, Gorbachev and his men put the blame on the leaders of the natives, and not the "Trojan horse" of Moscow in the republic. This is proven not only by the official news presented by the TASS agency about Gorbachev's meeting with the Soviet deputies on the part of the SSR of Moldavia. Ten days after the publication of this official news, which said that the tense nature of inter-ethnic relations in Moldavia are the result of the mistakes made by *the leadership of the republic* in the national policy, Gorbachev himself repeated the accusations against the leaders of the natives. Taking the floor during the fourth session of the Supreme Soviet of the USSR, and maintaining, among other things, that "some people ignore the existent realities" and try to "put forward a destructive idea from an economic, political, and human point of view," he exclaimed: "Here are our friends from Moldavia, I talked to some of them."[95]

A day before its publication this speech of the Soviet leader was presented on television (TV Moscow, 21 September 1990). At the words quoted above, the television operators showed on the screen the image of Gorbachev's "friends from Moldavia" among whom Iurii Blohin was present. After he proved, with the help of the television, who were his "friends from Moldavia," Gorbachev passed on to condemning those who were guilty, in his opinion, *of the mistakes in the policy promoted in Moldavia* that led to the situation that "the integrity of this generally compact, very dynamic, integrated republic is now being endangered."[96]

On 12 October 1990 the Soviet television transmitted Gorbachev's appeal toward *the deputies at all levels* from the SSR of Moldavia in which he asked them to find a way of reciprocal understanding for the détente of the extremely tense atmosphere within the republic. This appeal made toward *the deputies at all levels* without previously consulting the Parliament of the SSR of Moldavia proves once again that Gorbachev and his men carried on a policy of silencing the patriotic forces from the republic by

---

[95]Ibid., 22 September 1990.

[96]Ibid.

instigating the non-natives and the *Mankurts* against the parliament of the republic.

The Distortion of Certain Post-War Moldavian Realities

Characterizing Gorbachev on the day when he was awarded the Nobel Prize for Peace for the year 1990, Ilia Zemțov, who in the last years specialized in writing alleged documentary biographies of the post-Brezhnev Soviet leaders, declared in an interview that Mihail Gorbachev was "the greatest revolutionary of the twentieth century."[97]

A digression is necessary here. The biography of Chernenko written by Zemțov reflects also the period when Gorbachev's predecessor functioned, under Brezhnev's rule, in Moldavia. The pages dedicated to Chernenko's Moldavian period abound in fallacies which denote that Zemțov wrote his work on the basis of misleading information without knowing and without having studied the political situation in the republic during those years. Let us look at the following affirmation made by Cernenko's biographer:

"Cernenko had arrived from Russia and the traditional relations between Moldavia and Romania made him suspicious. He considered them to be a manifestation of nationalism, he was also indignant by the Latin alphabet of the Moldavian language: unintelligible and — the greatest danger — a Western influence could be felt in it. With his participation (Chernenko's) the writing changed to the Cyrillic alphabet."[98]

Only a man with no self-respect could affirm that Chernenko was suspicious regarding "the traditional relations between Moldavia and Romania," because these ties had been interrupted long before Moscow sent him to Moldavia in 1948. Another fallacy is Zemțov's assertion that Cernenko contributed to the changing of the natives's writing to the Cyrillic alphabet, and that, after this change, "Chernenko begins to feel more secure: as before he does not

---

[97] "Erev hadas," TV Israel, 15 October 1991.

[98] I. Zemtsov, *Chernenko. Sovetskii Soiuz v kanun perestroiki*. London, 1989, p. 47.

understand the language, but it looks less strange — those that are written can be read."[99]

If Chernenko's biographer had made the effort to read on this matter, he would have found out that the passing to the Cyrillic alphabet was done in the republic already in the first half of the year *1941*, while his hero first came in Moldavia only in *1948.*

According to Zemțov, despite the fact that Cernenko was not viewed favorably by the leadership of the republic and especially by N. Coval, the first secretary of the Central Committee, all the events that took place in the political, economic, and ideological life after his coming to Moldavia were to a great extent the result of his initiatives. Thus, Chernenko's biographer writes that "in 1949 in Moldavia began the process of discharging the Jews from leadership positions, and Chernenko's ideological apparatus was one of the first to be 'purified' of Jews." (p. 46). But the propaganda section had been purified of Jews long before Chernenko (a single Jew, Bukarsky, born on the left side of the Dniester, who was still a member of this section before Chernenko became its head, remained so long after the latter left the republic).

Also in flagrant contradiction with the truth are Zemțov's affirmations that at the beginning of April 1949 the head of the propaganda section of the Central Committee gave Iliașenco, his assistant, the task of organizing a meeting of the Writers's Union "whose agenda had undoubtedly been elaborated by Chernenko himself and reminded of the famous article from the newspaper *Sovetskaia Moldavia* (p. 46)." That article in which Chernenko accused the writers of the republic of "being incapable to see the exploiting essence of Romanian nationalism and to appreciate the civilizing mission of the Russian tsars."[100]

Chernenko, and not only him, but also the whole communist propaganda and Soviet historiography praised the "civilizing mission" of Russia and of the Russians, but never had Moscow and the *Mankurts* from the non-Russian territories attributed such a mission

---

[99] Ibid.

[100] I. Zemtsov, op. cit, p. 45.

to *the Russian tsars*, as Zemţov tries to convince us that Chernenko was doing in those years.

I made this digression because Zemţov judges Chernenko's successor also by appearances, by the impression he produces. But appearances are often deceptive. Viewed in the light of his real intentions, of the disguised and often even outspoken meaning of his declarations, of the policy promoted toward the non-Russian peoples of the vast empire, Gorbachev appears totally different from the leader who fascinated and still fascinates to a certain extent the West and the Sovietologists who, like Zemţov, do not make the effort (or are not interested) to base their estimations and conclusions on an objective analysis of the Gorbachev phenomenon. Such an analysis shows that, if we were to consider the Soviet leader in relation to the founders of scientific socialism (he always declared that he was a devoted follower of the socialist way of development of society), we should conclude that Gorbachev is not at all a revolutionary in the sense and spirit of Marx and Engels, but an opportunist lacking any principles.

"Reorganization and New Thinking for Our Country and for the Whole World"
(Theses, Formulas, Old-Fashioned Slogans)

Many of the key formulas of the "Perestroika" phenomenon which Gorbachev tried to substantiate in his work *Perestroika i novoe myshlenie dlia nashei strany i dlia vsego mira* (*Reorganization and New Thinking for Our Country and for the Whole World*)[101] succumbed a short time after they were put into circulation. I will insist on a few examples of Gorbachev's interpretation of the historical facts in the spirit of the stereotypes of Soviet propaganda from the time of his predecessors. Thus, in flagrant contradiction with the historical truth, Gorbachev maintains in his book that "the vitality of the plans elaborated by the party, which were understood and assimilated by the people, of the slogans and intentions based on

---

[101]M. Gorbachev, *Perestroika i novoe myshlenie dlia nashei strany i dlia vsego mira*. Moscow, 1987.

the energy of our revolution (the Revolution of October, 1917) found its expression in the amazing enthusiasm of millions of people who were drawn into the building up of the country's industry in extremely difficult conditions, often far from their homes,... with a wretched sustenance they were doing wonders. What was urging them on was the fact that they were participating in a magnificent historic realization... This was indeed a mass heroism for the future of the Country, a demonstration of the whole people's devotion toward the free choice that was made in 1917."[102]

The reorganization proclaimed by Gorbachev vehemently criticized the *semi-truth* which was resorted to during Brezhnev's rule to cover-up the negative aspects of Soviet realities. Despite the fact that it mentions "the extremely difficult conditions" in which the builders of the country's industry "did wonders," the fragment reproduced above is a succession not only of semi-truths, but also of falsehoods resorted to by the one who vehemently criticized semi-truths as a means of misleading the people. After the publication of Gorbachev's book, numerous publications *appeared in the USSR* which, based on documentary data, revealed the truth that "the mass heroism" was in fact a superhuman effort made by millions of people horrified by the Stalinist regime of terror; that not only young people influenced by the propaganda of party worked "far from their homes," but also millions of people deported by force.

However, we do not intend to point out here the numerous similar examples from Gorbachev's book, but rather the galloping manner in which the theses and key formulas used by the Soviet leader as a basis for the "reorganization" of Soviet Society were becoming obsolete. We will insist on a few examples from his book, some regarding his "new thinking" on the development of Soviet society (...*new thinking for our country*), others crossing the borders of the USSR (...*and for the whole world*). Thus, although in 1987 he categorically declared in his book: "Our program of reorganization, both on the whole, as well as in its various components, is based on the principle: more Socialism, more democracy,"[103] the key formula

---

[102]Ibid., p. 35.

[103]Ibid., p. 32.

"more socialism, more democracy" disappeared in a short time from the vocabulary of Gorbachev and his men.

The Soviet leader maintains the following facts in his book:

a) "the concept of economic reform which we elaborated and presented during the plenary session of June (1987) has a complex and all-embracing character, it does not leave any aspect of the problem without profound essential changes;"[104]

b) "the decisions (of the plenary session) accomplish the elaboration of the contemporary *model* of the socialist economy which corresponds to the actual stage in the development of our country."[105]

But the declaration that the decisions of the plenary session of June 1987 of the Central Committee *accomplished* the contemporary model of the socialist economy became obsolete as well, and subsequently Gorbachev was forced to maintain that "the socialist idea does not exclude the market economy,"[106] which he does not even mention in his book.

Also regarding the "new thinking on the further development of Soviet society" we should mention the assertion that "the reorganization began at the initiative of the Communist Party and develops under its guidance."[107]

Despite Gorbachev's resistance, articles 6 and 7 of the Constitution of the USSR, which proclaimed the leading role of the Communist party in the Soviet Union, were finally abrogated and official propaganda did not mention any longer the *leading role* of the Communist Party of the USSR, but its *influence*.

The events that took place in the Soviet republics after the publication of Gorbachev's book revealed in front of the whole world the unsubstantiality of his affirmations that: a) "the communion of (Soviet) peoples was formed on the basis of brotherhood and collaboration, of mutual respect and support;" that b) socialism "disposes of all the conditions necessary for resolving national

---

[104]Ibid., p. 82.

[105]Ibid., p. 85.

[106]*Pravda*, 26 October 1990.

[107]M. Gorbachev, *Perestroika*..., p. 52-53.

problems in the spirit of equality and collaboration among people;" that d) in the USSR "the national problem is in the main resolved."[108]

Many of the "fundamental" theses from those parts of Gorbachev's book that are dedicated to "the new thinking for the whole world" are also completely out-of-date. Thus, the Soviet leader's anticipation that "in the near future socialism, despite the prophecies of its enemies, will fully prove its inherent potential,"[109] that "revolutionary changes take place within the great international socialist home," that "although they (these changes) regard the socialist countries, they represent a contribution to the progress of civilization."[110] The changes that took place in the "great socialist home" after the elaboration of these theses were indeed revolutionary changes, but in a totally opposite sense to the one foreseen by the Soviet leader.

Karl Marx, whose statements are often quoted by Gorbachev in his book, said that when an author republishes his book, be it only after half a year, he must add certain specifications dictated by the events and phenomena that happened after the publication of the first edition. It is clear that Marx did not have in view radical changes dictated by the deliberate distorted presentation of the realities analyzed in the respective book. The numerous speeches made on different occasions show that, for an eventual republishing of *Reorganization and New Thinking...* Gorbachev would need not only to change completely numerous passages in his book, but also to renounce many key formulas and terms he used in his arguments.

The famous formula "friendship among peoples" used by the author of *Reorganization and New Thinking...* began to be bantered about even in the publications of the Communist Party.

It is not surprising that, in a question addressed to a participant at a "roundtable" organized within the "Rezonans" program of the Soviet television, a (Soviet) viewer characterized Gorbachev as "our

---

[108] Ibid., p. 118-119.

[109] Ibid., p. 176.

[110] Ibid.

man among strangers and stranger among his own people;"[111] "his own people" being here a contextual synonym for the population of the USSR. Being totally justified, this formula reflected at the same time the state of mind of the overwhelming majority of the non-Russian peoples from every Union republic who realized that Gorbachev was a continuer of the imperialist policy promoted by his predecessors. Thus, it is not surprising that, at the opening of the fourth Congress of People's Deputies of the USSR, the question of giving Gorbachev a vote of no confidence was raised.[112] The Stalinist-Brezhnevist majority of the deputies opposed this effort. Deputy V. Shapovalenko, as an exponent of this majority, asked for the nominal registering of the way the motion of no confidence against Gorbachev would be voted. There is no doubt that had the voting not been open, many or even very many weak-willed deputies would have voted differently. Secondly, even in these circumstances 609 deputies (426 voted in favor of the motion and 183 and abstained from voting), that is 32% of those who participated in the voting, did not support Gorbachev. Thirdly, another 10% of all the deputies in general did not present themselves at the Congress, as they considered that, by the "new Union Convention" Gorbachev was trying to perpetuate Moscow's domination over the non-Russian peoples of the Soviet Empire.

To counteract the efforts of the natives of some non-Russian Soviet republics, especially of the Baltic republics, to declare their territories free and independent states, Gorbachev repeatedly used the argument that a new union convention was being elaborated, the adoption of which would ensure the true sovereignty of the Soviet states, that the Soviet peoples had not yet lived in a federation of truly sovereign states. The publication in November 1990 of the project of the highly praised new Union Convention led, however, to an even greater discrediting of the Soviet leader in the eyes of the patriotic masses from the non-Russian republics of the USSR. Article 5 of the new Union Convention, with all its eight paragraphs plus the conclusion that "the prerogatives of the Union can not be changed

---

[111] TV Moscow, 12 April 1990.

[112] *Izvestia*, 18 December 1990.

without the consent of all the republics," Article 9 which dealt with the supremacy of the laws regarding the composition of the USSR and the obligation of observing them on the territory of each republic, as well as Article 19 which stipulated that "the Russian language, that has become the language of inter-ethnic communication, is recognized by the participants in the Convention as the state language of the USSR" show that Gorbachev had no intention of renouncing the domination of the non-Russian Soviet peoples, that the advocated introduction of the term "sovereign" instead of "socialist" in the name of the Union of the Soviet Socialist Republics was only a palliative, a new way of disguising the real essence of the Soviet Empire. In fact, as if warning Gorbachev not to carry things too far, the Stalinist-Brezhnevist majority of the Congress voted against the introduction in the name of the USSR of the term "sovereign."

It is not surprising that the ever stronger deviation toward the establishing of a dictatorial regime within the USSR generated, on the one hand, fierce internal struggles among the native population of the non-Russian Soviet republics, between the patriots and the *Mankurts*, the latter enjoying the full support of Gorbachev's Moscow and of the majority of Russophones from these republics. On the other hand, the danger of the establishment of a dictatorial regime led also to internal conflicts among the Russians in their Union republic, Gorbachev's adversaries asking more and more insistently for his dismissal from the position of president of the USSR.

PART II

FROM THE COLLAPSE OF THE SOVIET EMPIRE (USSR) TO THE REORGANIZATION OF THE RUSSIAN EMPIRE (CIS)

I. BETWEEN A ROCK AND A HARD PLACE

Romanianophobia Disguised as Regional Patriotism

In my work *Rossia, Rumania i Bessarabia*[1] (*Russia, Romania, and Bessarabia*) I repeatedly mentioned that the Bessarabian Moldavians, an integral part of the dominant nation in the period 1918-1940, did not sympathize, in their majority, with the communists, especially because the latter were infringing upon the territorial integrity of the Romanian state, their main objective being to help Moscow take control over Bessarabia.

At the same time, we pointed out that during the years 1918-1940 the communist organization in Bessarabia was numerically a marginal movement, supported, understandably, by representatives of the national minorities[2] and animated by Moscow's agents infiltrated in the country.

Analyzing the national policy promoted by the Communist Party in Soviet Moldavia,[3] I wrote that although the participants in the underground communist movement in Bessarabia during the years

---

[1] Michael Bruchis, *Rossia, Rumania i Bessarabia*, Tel Aviv, 1979, p. 292 and passim.

[2] Ibid., p. 300 and passim.

[3] Michael Bruchis, *Nation — Nationalities — People*, Boulder-New York, 1984.

1918-1940 were in their overwhelming majority representatives of the national minorities (Russians, Ukrainians, and Jews), within these minorities the communists and their sympathizers represented a totally negligible numerical entity, the bulk of the Bessarabian non-Romanian population did not take part in and did not support the subversive actions of the communists.[4]

The book *Russia, Romania, and Bessarabia* was conceived as a pleading for the historical rights of Romania over the territories of the Romanian people taken over by Tsarist Russia in 1812 and by Soviet Russia in 1940. And the non-Romanian nationalities living in Bessarabia during the years 1918-1940 were not characterized in the book as oppressed nationalities on the whole. The epithet *oppressed* appears in *Russia, Romania, and Bessarabia* in a certain combination of words, namely: "*the most oppressed strata of the non-Moldavian population*" (*predstaviteli naibolee ugnetennykh nemoldavskikh sloev naselenia*).[5] There is a substantial, fundamental difference between "*the oppressed strata*" and "*the oppressed nationalities*," not only because in the respective text we affirm that the communist underground from Bessarabia was recruiting its members "especially from among the representatives of the most oppressed strata of the non-Moldavian population."[6] The word *especially* can only indicate here that for the Bessarabian communists the most favorable group from which to recruit their partisans was that of the *most oppressed strata* of the national minorities and not the latter as a whole.

Țurcanu's statement that the Bessarabian Romanians (the Moldavians) were not *representatives of the dominant nation* of the country in the period 1918-1940 as "the Moldavian peasants, that is the Romanians,... this large mass of people, were living in very difficult conditions, working to exhaustion," derives from his feelings of sympathy toward *the oppressed strata* of his people under the regime of the respective period. This does not mean, however, that the Bessarabian Romanians as an ethnic community native of the

---

[4]Ibid., p. 184.

[5]Michael Bruchis, *Rossia, Rumania i Bessarabia*, p. 246.

[6]Ibid.

province were not part of the dominant nation of the country, that they did not become an integral part of the dominant nation of Romania, and thus representatives of this *dominant nation*.

The fact that significant strata of the *dominant nation* had reasons to be dissatisfied with the difficult living conditions during the period 1918-1940 refers a totally different aspect of the inter-war Romanian realities, namely the economic and social-political situation of Romanian society of that time, and not inter-ethnic relations. Saying that a certain ethnic community, taken as a whole, is *the dominant nation* of a multinational state implies the fact that representatives of that particular ethnic community hold key positions in all the vitally important spheres of activity in the country: the administration, the army, justice, etc.

For example, the Russians, in their majority, lived in very difficult conditions not only under the Tsarist regime, but also under the Soviet one. However, taken as a whole, as an ethnic community, they were all *representatives of the dominant nation*, both under the Tsarist regime, as well as under the communist one, not only on the territory of Russia proper, but also on the vast territories of the peoples subdued by Moscow over the centuries. More than that, although in most of these territories the Russians were numerically a *minority*, sometimes a totally negligible one in relation to the natives, as *representatives of the dominant nation* of the Tsarist and respectively Soviet Empire they held key positions in each of the subdued territories.

We can say that the Romanians, in contrast with what the Russians did in 1812, did not subdue the natives of Bessarabia in 1918, but they helped their Bessarabian brothers to defend their legitimate right to national self-determination and, finally, to join with Romania the lands which had been occupied by Moscow in 1812. All these statements are in agreement with the historical truth regarding the essence of both the events of 1812 as well as of 1918. But they do no mean that, after the events of 1918, the Bessarabian Romanians *did not change from an oppressed national minority within the Russian Empire into a natural part of the dominant nation of the Romanian state*. The events of 1918 were reflected by the fact that, through the unification of Bessarabia, Bucovina, and Transylvania with Romania, the native population of these ancient Romanian territories became an integral part of the *dominant nation* of Greater Romania. A direct consequence of these events and an edifying manifestation of the new state of affairs in Bessarabia, for instance, was that it was not the Russians, but the Romanians, including the Bessarabian Romanians, who held key positions in the Bessarabian administration, education, justice, etc. during the period 1918-1940.

Among the officials who during this period held key positions in the important fields of activity in Bessarabia there were also Romanians who were natives of other provinces of the Romanian Kingdom. This indisputable fact is presented in the studies of the obedient Soviet historians as "incontestable evidence" that "the bourgeois-landlord Romania subdued the Moldavian people in 1918" and that the USSR liberated it in 1940. Nowadays, however, some of these historians suddenly changed their position. Anton Moraru, for instance, wrote in an article entitled "Contribuții la istoria formării R.S.S. Moldovenești" ("Contributions to the formations of the SSR of Moldavia") that "on 3 July 1940 the Central Committee approved the composition of the district committees of the Ukrainian Communist Party in Soviet Bessarabia and Northern Bucovina. These district committees included: I.S. Grușciețki, T.A. Constantinov, N.S. Krușnii, A.X. Karapîs, I.I. Pojidaiev, A.N. Nicolaiev, S.I. Antoniuk, V.P. Lîmari, G.M. Kulîghin, N.N. Pecerski, P.V. Orlenko, N.A. Trofimenko, and others. Among them there were only two Moldavians: T.A. Constantinov and S.S. Zelenciuc, and there were no natives of Bessarabia... Of the 75 members of the executive district committees, 71 were Russians and Ukrainians and only two were Moldavians."[7]

The data which A. Moraru refers to proves how unfounded were the attacks addressed by him and other obedient Soviet historians to those who were writing in the West that with the occupation of Bessarabia in 1940 the Moldavian republic created by Moscow had been invaded by foreigners who occupied all the key positions.[8]

---

[7] A. Moraru, "Contribuții la istoria formării R.S.S. Moldovenești," L. Bulat (ed.), *Basarabia 1940*. Kishinev, 1991, pp. 160-161.

[8] S. Brysiakin, M. Satnic, *Triumful adevărului istoric*. Chișinău, 1970; A. Moraru, *Otpoved' fal'sifikatoram*, Chișinău, 1981, and passim.

The foreigners were, in fact, also those *Transnistrian Moldavians* who, after the occupation of Bessarabia by Moscow, were named as heads of the educational, cultural, and scientific institutions because *most of them* were *Mankurts*, speaking a jargon which they were trying to impose on the Moldavians as a literary language, and promoters of an obscurant theory regarding the origins, history, language, and literature of the Romanians east of the Prut.

But the Romanians outside Bessarabia, both those who were there in 1917-1918, as well as those who settled there in the next years until 1940 cannot be considered foreigners. First of all, they were not only of the same blood as the Bessarabian Romanians (the Moldavians east of the Dniester were also of the same blood), but they spoke the Romanian literary language, contributing to the regeneration of the national language of the Bessarabian Romanians. Secondly, regardless of what part of the Romanian state they were from, those Romanians outside Bessarabia who were functioning in it (and in Bucovina as well) in the educational, cultural, and scientific fields brought with them the truth about the origins, history, language, and literature of the people to which the Bessarabian (and Bucovinian) Romanians belonged. The opposition between the Transnistrian Romanians, *foreign* to the lands occupied by Moscow in 1940, who brought with them slogans and theories foreign to their people, and the Romanians from any part of the country except Bessarabia (and Bucovina), who brought with them during the period 1918-1940 the historical truth and contributed to the regeneration of the language found its artistic reflection in the work of the great Bessarabian Romanian writer Ion Druță. Both the heroes and the descriptions of Ion Druță truthfully reflected Bessarabian realities in the past as well as in the Soviet period. We could mention other writers who, during those years, had the courage to criticize in one or even in many of their writings the realities of Soviet Moldavia: Grigore Vieru, P. Cărare, V. Vasilache, A. Busuioc, Gheorghe Cutasevici, and others. But Druță was undoubtedly the pioneer of protest literature during that period, his work serving as a model of great artistic value for younger generations.

The majority of the members of the Writers's Union were not guided in their work by the realities of the republic. Their writings were usually in flagrant disagreement with these realities, reflecting the slogans and theories put forward by the promoters of the official Soviet policy. For the heroes of such writings the country lies from the Prut to Vladivostok. The authors in this category generalized certain sporadic facts and events that did not reflect the state of mind of Bessarabian society as a whole, but just some marginal manifestations.

These manifestations, animated and supported by Moscow during the period 1918-1940, being marginal, did not represent a great danger to the Romanian state from a domestic view point. But they represented a serious danger for Romania from an international stand point because Moscow used them to provide communist, pro-communist, and pro-Soviet circles with propaganda material in support of its attempts to take over Bessarabia, and to mislead international public opinion about the aspirations of the majority of the Bessarabian population in preparation for an eventual occupation of the province by Soviet troops.

For the heroes of Ion Druță, however, *the country lies from the Dniester to the Tisa*. Although the position of some of these writers was not always consistent, many of their writings, despite the efforts of the obedient historiography and linguistics, were awakening the sentiments and aspirations of the patriotic native population, especially of the intellectuals and the students.

During the Soviet regime from July 1940 to July 1941, all of the Bessarabian writers were eyewitnesses to realities such as massive deportations, imprisonment, and even massacres of innocent people, including writers and scholars. All of these events frightened them so much that nothing remained of the courage they had manifested within the Romanian state. This explains the fact that most of the Bessarabian poets and writers did not dare protest openly against the change over to the Cyrillic alphabet in Bessarabia, although they continued to write in Romanian and some of the Bessarabian poets wrote their poems using the Latin alphabet, and only afterwards transposed them into the Cyrillic alphabet for publication. The change that took place in the attitude of Bessarabian writers under the Soviet regime in relation with their attitude under the Romanian regime is undeniable proof that the former was a regime of terror, compared to which the inter-war Romanian regime, when Bessarabia was part of the Romanian state, was a tolerant one.

The publicist Nicolae Bătrînu wrote, in October 1991, that together with "the great writers and scholars of Romania" who came after the events of 1918 "to the liberated provinces to hold out their hands to their freed brothers, to listen to their wishes and sorrows," there also crossed "the borders of the liberated provinces the opportunists of the Romanian state: gendarmes and tax collectors, banal lawyers and greedy politicians, who cared more about their own interests than about the good of the country," so that after years of Romanian regime "the great-grandparents and the grandparents" of the natives were asking themselves at that time, as their great-grandchildren and grandchildren are asking themselves now: "Was this the purpose of our sufferings and oppressions under foreigners, so that our brothers from across the Prut and from below the Carpathians could come now and make fun of us, the Bessarabians, the Bucovinians, and the Transylvanians?"[9]

We should also mention here the transparent *generalization* made by Bătrînu according to which in our days the majority of the Romanians from Romania are "occasional patriots," and the majority of the Romanians who live in the West "have cried out loudly for the last 50 years that they miss their country," but they have no intention of coming back to it.

Nowadays, the animosity toward the Romanians (both from Romania as well as from other countries) which penetrates through Nicolae Bătrînu's article is sustained, on the one hand, by the fact that some of them set themselves up as mentors (some citizens of the Romanian state), and others try to gain personal profits from their ties with the republic (some visitors from Western countries). But in Bătrînu's article this animosity aims, in fact, at *the great majority* of the Romanians outside Bessarabia. This is why such articles are not only detrimental, but they are also based on misleading premises, as the greatest part of the Romanians from Romania and from the West have the most sincere sentiments toward their Bessarabian brothers.

This animosity, generated by an exaggerated *local patriotism*, materializes in some publications into intolerance toward the representatives of the non-Romanian population of the republic, and

---

[9]*Literatura şi Arta*, 31 October 1991.

in such cases this *local patriotism* takes the form of manifestations of *chauvinistic nationalism*.

Both the period that followed in Bessarabia after the Unification of 1918, as well as the one which, in the SSR of Moldavia, followed the great accomplishments of the Romanians east of the Prut in 1989 in saving their mother tongue, the return to the Latin alphabet, and the national symbols (the tricolor flag) were unfortunately accompanied by fierce internal, *inter*-Romanian fights.

After the realization of the aspirations of the Bessarabian Romanians, who in 1918 (after more than a century of foreign rule) became an integral part of the dominant nation of the country, many of the militants who fought with abnegation for the self-determination of the Bessarabian population and for unification with Romania "let themselves be drawn — as Octavian Ghibu asserts — in the party policy, ...defending group interests even when they were aware that they were defending a wrong cause, they offended and abused one another."[10]

The insults and abuses which embitter the *inter*-Romanian atmosphere in the Republic of Moldavia in our days, unlike those which our predecessors resorted to, broke out *before the country could be reunified*, and they endanger the possibility of carrying out the centuries-old dream of the most enlightened minds of the Romanian people. Regarding this sad reality, Nicolae Dabija writes: "We are at war with each other, while our enemies stand by and laugh at us."[11] Dabija, one of the animators of Romanianism in the republic, uses, of course, a figure of speech when he says that "our enemies stand by and laugh at us." In his article ("La un pas sau la o veşnicie de unire,"[12]) he reproduces a "sentence," < Obştii 'Memorie' > , which shows that the enemies of the Romanians *do not by any means stand by and laugh*, but terrorize, instigate, and breed dissension. By the respective "sentence," dated 15 December 1989 and written in an incorrect Romanian language which indicates that

---

[10]*Literatura şi Arta*, 7 November 1991.

[11]Ibid., 5 December 1991.

[12]Ibid.

it is a bad translation after a text which was conceived and written in Russian, "the following citizens are condemned to death: 1. Nicolae Dabija, 2. Grigore Vieru, 3. L. Iorga (Leonida Lari)."

Although the inspirers of the "death sentence" pronounced it allegedly "in the name of all the peoples that live on the territories of the SSR of Moldavia,"[13] thus posing as friends of the whole population of the republic, they are in fact enemies of the natives who are trying to perpetuate the latter's situation as a subdued ethnic group on the territory of their own people. And, regardless of who were the inspirers of the sentence, the non-Romanians or the *Mankurts*, the Romanian patriots are entitled to expose them to the public contempt. The founders of the ideology of those who pretend to act "in the name of *all the peoples* that live on the territory of the SSR of Moldavia" to protect their vital interests were Iurii Blohin, V. Iacovlev, A. Lisetky, V. Stati, and others. They fought fiercely both against the declaration of the natives's language as state language, as well as against the return to the national symbols of the Romanians on the left side of the Prut, inventing all kinds of arguments in favor of maintaining the Cyrillic alphabet. Iurii Blohin, deputy of the Supreme Soviet of the USSR on the part of the Republic of Moldavia, became one of the principal spokesmen of the parliamentary bloc "Soiuz" whose objective was to save at any price the Soviet Empire and Russian domination on its whole territory; V. Iacovlev, deputy of the Supreme Soviet of Moldavia, proved to be one of the ideologists of the dismemberment of the republic and the creation of the so-called Autonomous Nistrian Moldavian Republic; A. Lisetsky, deputy of the Supreme Soviet of the republic, began to declare himself against the separatists in Tiraspol and Comrat. All these people laid the foundations of the "Edinstvo" movement in the republic. Despite the differences in the evolution of the position of each of these ideologists of the *Mankurts* and Russophones, they remained supporters of maintaining Moldavia under Moscow's domination. Even if they were not among those who edited the pamphlet containing the death sentence of the patriotic poets Grigore Vieru, Nicolae Dabija, and Leonida Lari "for the systematic and

---

[13]Ibid.

malignant instigation of inter-ethnic hostility,"[14] as initiators, inspirers, and leaders of the Russophones and *Mankurts* they are morally responsible through their essentially anti-Romanian activity for generating the appearance of such criminal instigations.

At the end of November 1991 Moscow Television transmitted an interview given by Eduard Shevardnadze to a Soviet journalist. The latter asked him, among other things, how could he explain the fact that, after he had been for years an activist in the Communist Party of the Soviet Union, holding positions of great responsibility within state and party bodies, he suddenly renounced communist ideology and became one of the leaders of the movement for democratic reform. Shevardnadze answered that an artist — a sculptor, a painter, a writer, or a composer —, after being a follower of a certain artistic trend for years, at a certain moment in his evolution can choose a different way of expressing himself and become not only a follower of a different trend, but even the leader of a new school. The same thing, he said, could also happen with a politician who, after he belonged for a period to a certain political party, could change his position, his political conception, and choose a different way to achieve his objectives and his aspirations within a different party.

Such a parallel is not, however, plausible. A real talent, a follower of a certain artistic school, is convinced that within the precepts that distinguish this school from others he will be able to express in a better way his artistic conception and his talent. Such an artist becomes a follower of a different trend when he realizes that he can no more bring into being his creative capacities within the trend whose follower he was before.

Shevardnadze's parallel is not only unfounded, but also deliberately misleading, because an artist with self-respect adheres to one or another trend even if this trend is not the dominant one at that time. And when such an artist shares, at a certain moment in his evolution, the principles and methods of a different trend, his new artistic orientation is the natural result of this evolution and not the fact that this other trend becomes the dominant one in art.

---

[14]Ibid.

This parallel would be well-founded, however, if we took into consideration such writers as Gheorghe Malarciuc, who tried for years to suggest to his readers that the overwhelming majority of the Romanians east of the Prut fought against the bourgeois-landlord Romanian state for the establishment of the Bolshevik power in Bessarabia, or such historians as Anatolii Lisetsky who supported for years the national policy promoted in the republic by the Communist Party and encouraged the degree candidates under his scientific guidance to write dissertations that supported the thesis that the Moldavian republic was developing within the "brotherly family" of Soviet peoples as a sovereign state on the basis of the free self-determination of the Moldavian people.

In time, Anatolii Lisetsky became, at first sight, one of the less aggressive propagators of Romanianophobia. In fact, however, his activity was no less dangerous for the existence of the native population of the republic as a Romanian national-ethnic entity than that of V. Iacovlev, the ideologist of the separatists from Tiraspol.

In one of his articles entitled "Natsional'nye men'shinstva: aspekty zakonotvorcheskogo protsessa" ("National minorities: aspects of a legislative process")[15] published in eight consecutive numbers of the newspaper *Nezavisimaia Moldova*, Lisetsky declares that he elaborated the draft bill regarding the national minorities of the republic as a result of his concern "for the interests of the Russophone population and of the whole people of Moldavia. The fact that the author of the article considers the Russophone population as part of the *whole people of Moldavia* is proved by the assertion that "regardless of the name of the draft bill — regarding national groups or national minorities — it concerns the vital interests not only of the 36% of the non-Moldavian population, but also of the whole population of the state," that is of the Republic of Moldavia. Considering the Russophone population as part of the whole people of Moldavia, Lisetsky maintains that "the usage (in the text of the law regarding the national minorities) of the term 'native' referring only

---

[15] A. Lisetsky, "Natsional'nye men'shinstva: aspekty zakonotvorcheskogo protsessa," in *Nezavisimaia Moldova*, 27, 28, 29, 31 October, 3, 4, 5, 7 November 1992.

to Moldavians is very vulnerable." He bases his affirmation on the following argument: "In the Republic of Moldavia not only the Moldavians are natives, but also those representatives of the other nationalities who have been living on this territory throughout many or a few generations." For this reason, writes Lisetsky, "we introduced (in his draft bill) the notion *titular nation* for the nation that gives the name of the state," and he adds that "from this point of view it (the notion) establishes the natural priority of the Moldavian people."

The way in which Lisetsky uses, on the one hand, the term *the Moldavian people* and, on the other hand, the expression *the whole people of Moldavia* denotes the fact that he considers the "national minorities" of Moldavia *on the whole*, regardless of their ethnic origin, as integral part of *the whole people of Moldavia*, but not of the *Moldavian people*. The priority of the Moldavian people is, in fact, idle talk, because Lisetsky is not concerned *with the vital interests of the Moldavian people*, but with the interests of the national minorities, and not of all the national minorities, but only of the Russians who live in Moldavia. When he claims that "every man should have the right to learn and use the language of his own people or of a part of his people," he is not concerned with any *priority of the Moldavian people* and not even *of the whole people of Moldavia*, but only with *the priority of the Russians from Moldavia as part of their own people, namely the Russian people*.

What concerns people like Lisetsky is that *the language of the whole people of Moldavia*, in other words the Russian language, continue to be used and that the state language of the republic not be mandatory for anyone.

We can say that the dissensions and especially the internal fights among the patriotic natives provide favorable conditions for the *Mankurts* and the Lisetsky type of "friends" of the Romanians east of the Prut.

Active Allies and Reserve Allies of Russian Imperialism

Those representatives of the Russian people who were in power in the vast Tsarist Empire and, after 1917, in the Soviet Empire perseveringly promoted within these empires a policy of denationalization and Russification of the non-Russian peoples subdued by Moscow over the centuries.

The slogans which Gorbachev used after his coming to power, in mid-1980s, led, contrary to his real intentions, to a rapid awakening of the self-awareness of the non-Russian Soviet peoples. The national consciousness of these peoples was directed by their intellectuals toward a series of claims that were vital for their ethnic existence as, first of all, the declaration of the non-Russian national language of the natives from each Soviet republic as state languages in their respective republics.

In Soviet Moldavia the struggle of patriotic intellectuals to defend their national language and reinstate the Latin alphabet from the very beginning encountered fierce opposition from the Russian population of the republic and, to a great extent, from the Russophone non-Russian population, as well as of the *Mankurts*.[16] The latter had propagated and continued to propagate, to the detriment of their own people, the national policy promoted by the Communist Party, praising, among other things, the so-called flourishing of the Moldavian language during the years of Soviet domination.

The opposition of the Russians and the *Mankurts* was even more vehement as both realized they were losing ground. The Russians, being aware that the process of regeneration of the fundamental national values of the natives, especially their language which was proclaimed the state language of the republic, could ultimately lead to their losing their dominant position in the political, economic, and cultural life of the republic, to their transformation from members of the dominant nation of the Soviet Empire into representatives of a national minority within a state which was moving further away from Moscow and drawing nearer and nearer to the country of Romanians from all lands, Romania.

---

[16]The word *Mankurt* was put into circulation by the writer Cinghiz Aitmatov, having the meaning of "someone who denies their own people." This term reflected an objective reality generated by the policy promoted by Moscow in absolutely all the non-Russian Soviet republics. This is why it took root in the vocabulary of the patriotic forces in these republics.

The emergence of the "Edinstvo" movement and the political strikes at industrial plants in Tiraspol, Râbnița, Tighina, and Bălți resulted from attempts by the representatives of the Russian strata of the republic's population to oppose the efforts of the patriotic native intellectuals to save their national language and, implicitly, their ethnic existence as part of the Romanian people.

The process of revival of national consciousness among the natives in the non-Russian Soviet republics was reflected in the proclamation of the respective national languages as official languages. Under these circumstances, in an attempt to calm the hundreds of thousands of Russians infiltrated in the non-Russian republics, and to reverse the consequences of the changing of the status of the languages of these republics, a law entitled "Regarding the Languages of the Peoples of the USSR" was adopted by Moscow. This law stipulated that "the Russian language is declared the official language on the territory of the USSR and used as a means of inter-ethnic communication for the purpose of union among the republics."

Moscow's strategy, meant to perpetuate, through the law adopted on 24 April 1990, Russian domination in the vast Soviet Empire and to further stimulate the Russification of the non-Russian peoples, was too transparent and it naturally provoked indignation among the patriotic intelligentsia in the respective republics. In the Republic of Moldavia, for example, the publication of the famous law signed by Gorbachev on 24 April 1990, led over 300 professors and students of the Medical Institute in Chișinău to express their profound indignation, declaring that "to decree the Russian language the official language is an act of discrimination toward other peoples and other national languages."[17]

The law "Regarding the Languages of the Peoples of the USSR" had repercussions also among the bloc of Russians, Russophones, and *Mankurts*, finally leading their break-up. Thus, one of the most active and aggressive promoters of the internationalist policy, university professor Anatolii Lisetsky, realizing that through the law of 24 April the Russians and the Russophones of the republic would not need to learn and use the state language of the republic in their professional

---

[17] *Literatura și Arta*, 24 May 1990.

and public activity, began to detach himself from the extremists of the "Edinstvo" movement. On the other hand, the internationalist Vasilii Iakovlev, also a professor at the University of Chișinău, never stopped his campaign against the legitimate claims of the Romanians east of the Prut, not even after the adoption of the law of 24 April. A short time later, Iacovlev became rector of the University founded by the separatists in Tiraspol and a fervent ideologist of the so-called Moldavian Nistrian Republic. In this position Iakovlev raged against the leaders of the Republic of Moldavia and maintained that both the Bessarabian and the Transnistrian Moldavians are not Romanians and that their language is different from Romanian. If we add here that the Russians and the *Mankurts* like Smirnov, Maracuța, Iakovlev named their so-called republic *Pridnestrovskaia moldavskaia avtonomnaia respublika*, the objectives of their policy become very clear. Thus, although the total number of Romanians living on the territory on the left side of the Dniester River represents less than 40% of the total population, and although only part of them, that is the totally Russified part, support the separatist Russians and Russophones from Tiraspol, the latter try to create the illusion that the so-called Nistrian Republic is a *Moldavian state*.

Not only the position Iakovlev and others like him, but also the position of people like Lisetsky (despite the fact that the latter began to detach himself from his former internationalist comrades, declaring himself categorically against the separatists) is in flagrant contradiction with the national interests of the Romanians east of the Prut.

Anatolii Lisetsky seemed to be the least aggressive of the initiators of the Romanianophobia, and not only did he declare himself against the separatists from Tiraspol and Comrat, but he also tried to give the impression of a level-headed politician who defended the vital interests of the whole population of the republic, regardless of the ethnic origin of the people. However, Lisetsky's metamorphosis did not affect in any way the essence of his position as spokesman for the Russophones, especially the Russians, who try to perpetuate Moscow's domination in the Republic of Moldavia and to prevent in any way the latter's union with Romania.

Thus, in one of his articles, Lisetsky criticized Vasilii Iacovlev, his former internationalist comrade, resorting to epithets which not long ago both of them would use to characterize the Western scientists who "dared" to reveal the true essence of Soviet realities in general and of those in the Republic of Moldavian in particular. In this article, Lisetsky vehemently attacked not only Vasilii Iakovlev, but also such ideologists of Soviet imperialism as Blohin, Alksnis, Petruşenco, and Jirinovsky. The arguments, assertions, hypotheses, and solutions of Lisetsky denote that he is not a man of principle, but an eclectic and an opportunist.

Regarding the realities specific to the Republic of Moldavia, Lisetsky declared, among other things:

a) the consolidation of the whole people of the Republic of Moldavia is needed at present;

b) the Russophones must not interfere in the question "Moldavians or Romanians?" leaving the Moldavian people to resolve it.[18]

These two statements, however, are only idle talk meant to disguise the cornerstones of his article. Thus, using in the first assertion the term *the whole people of the Republic of Moldavia* and in the other the term *the Moldavian people*, Lisetsky is trying to prove the thesis that there is a *whole people of Moldavia, the only people*, and that *the Moldavian people is only a constituent part of this people*. The badly dissimulated hidden meaning of the usage of the term *the only people* is even more evident in a different passage of his article where he uses the formula "the relations between the two linguistic communities historically constituted." In this passage Lisetsky maintains that "the process of Moldavia's becoming an independent state depends on the relations between the two linguistic communities historically constituted on its territory."[19]

We could use the term *linguistic communities historically constituted* for those communities from Switzerland or even Belgium, because the ancestors of the nowadays representatives of such communities settled hundreds or thousands of years ago on neighboring territories which throughout history became integral parts of a certain state. A large part of the Russophones and the majority of the Russians on the territory on the left side of the Prut do not

---

[18]A. Lisetsky, "Uroki gosudartsvennogo perevorota," in *Sovetskaia Moldavia*, 22 November 1992.

[19]Ibid., p. 3.

have centuries-old roots in Moldavia, not even in Transnistria. Besides, we should consider here the fact that the linguistic community of the Russophones that appeared on the territories of the Romanians east of the Prut is not the result of a natural historical evolution, but of a premeditated policy of systematic denationalization and Russification of the natives, promoted here by the Russian invaders both under the Tsarist regime as well as, at a more rapid pace, under the Soviet regime. This is why the word combination "the two linguistic communities constituted *historically*" is a euphemistic formulation used by Lisetsky to dissimulate somehow the truth that one of these communities *did not constitute,* but *was constituted* after taking over of the territory belonging to the other.

If the evolution of events will bring "the relations between the two linguistic communities" to a turning point, in the sense that, unlike in the past, not the Russian language but the Romanian language will extend more and more its social functions in the republic, the majority of Russians, like Lisetsky, will renounce the formula "the only people of Moldavia." They will appeal, like I. Smirnov and Vasilii Iakovlev are doing today in Transnistria, to their countrymen from Russia proper and form their empire which still exists on the vast territories of the Russian Federation. They will ask for help from all those who will have "remorse" because "their countrymen are offended, being separated from their people by new frontiers." The generals, foremost of whom Pavel Graciov and the military units armed to the teeth under the command of Lebed and the Cossacks from the most various regions of the empire (today called the Russian Federation or simply Russia) who are overrunning the self-proclaimed Nistrian Republic to support the separatists from Tiraspol, all are the reserve allies of the Russians from the colonies of the former USSR, from the so-called "*blijnee zarubejie,*" a term put into circulation after Gorbachev's removal, meaning "the neighboring territories from across the actual frontiers of the Russian Empire."

The reserve allies of the Russians on the right side of the Dniester, who today declare themselves against the territorial dismemberment of the republic, can become overnight active allies of those like Lisetsky, as they are now the active allies of Vasilii Iakovlev, I. Smirnov, and the other separatists from Tiraspol. The following events serve to support this affirmation. Thus, in the second half of May 1992, when the 14th Army openly passed on the side of the separatists from Tiraspol, Mircea Snegur was forced to protest in front of the United Nations against Russia's aggression and to warn them that, in case that Russia would not cease its military intervention, the Republic of Moldavia would have to declare war.

The immediate response of Boris Yeltsin was that the 14th Army would retreat from the territory of Transnistria. But this declaration proved to be idle talk, because soon after that, Pavel Graciov, the Russian Minister of Defence, brought a corrective to the president's declaration that changed its very essence. In an interview he gave to Andrei Scriabin, the correspondent for Moscow television, Graciov, answering a question related to the above-mentioned declaration of Russia's President, confirmed that the retreat of the 14th Army was decided, but he added right away that it was not a matter of an immediate retreat, that first of all the political problems caused, as he said, "by the mistakes of Moldavia's leadership" had to be resolved. And a few days after, the same general declared that he would put Russia's military forces into action in case that it would be necessary to defend Russians living in the CIS republics.[20]

Historical Fatherland and Adoptive Fatherland

In the present socio-political conditions of the republic it is not at all surprising that those who pull the strings in the camp of the internationalist Mankurts, as well as those of the ultra-patriots began a new wave of denigrations against the "renegade" Bruchis who allegedly:

a) asks insolently for the disintegration of the Republic of Moldavia, and supports the separatists;

b) "considers that the Transnistrian Romanians do not have the right to be citizens of an integrated Moldavia, and recommends that the Bessarabian Romanians not annex the Transnistrian lands to Bessarabia, but leave them in the composition of the Ukraine;

---

[20]TV Moscow, 5 June 1992.

c) "directly addresses the publishing houses of Moldavia with the proposition: publish my books. This call was heard, one of his books... appeared in the pages of *Basarabia* magazine," etc.[21]

To make a detailed analysis of the calumnies directed against me (based on terms used out of context and on falsifications) I would need many pages of commentary. This is why I will take into consideration only a few of Nircă's falsifications and two or three terms he uses out of context. Thus, *the disintegration* of the *Autonomous* Moldavian Republic was done by Moscow through the law of 2 August 1940, when the *disintegration* of Bessarabia was also committed (after its annexation at the end of June 1940). What I maintain is that Transnistria is not a historical land of the Romanians, just as Northern Bucovina is not a historical land of the Ukrainians, as Transylvania is not a historical land of the Hungarians, and as Bessarabia is not a historical land of the Gagauz. But one could never find in any of my writings that "*the Transnistrian Romanians do not have the right to be citizens of an integrated Moldavia.*"

The term *separatists* used in the first passage reproduced from Nircă's article ("Bruchis... supports the separatists") is in a certain respect from the same category as the term *an integrated Moldavia*, in the sense that in the conception of people like Nircă *integrated* Moldavia represents the disintegrated Bessarabia of 1940, to which Moscow annexed six (of the fourteen) districts of the dissolved autonomous republic.

To the above I must add the following:

In my work *Nation — Nationalities — People* (1984) I wrote that the activists of the communist underground in Bessarabia maintained in their propaganda that during an interrogation the investigator shouted at engineer A. Rubinstein (the ideologist of the Bessarabian communists during the period 1918-1940) "To Palestine with you, or to Russia," and that the latter replied him: "This is where we were born and lived all our life,... let the uncalled for foreigners leave, who stay here by force of bayonets."[22]

---

[21] E. Nirca, "Bişniţar politic," in *Moldova Suverană*, 18 September 1991.

[22] Michael Bruchis, *Nations — Nationalities — People*, p. 165.

The possibility of such a reply is not at all out of the question. "To Palestine with the Jews" was a slogan frequently used by the anti-Semites during the period 1918-1940. In *Nation — Nationalities — People* we commented upon the alleged reply:

"Rubinstein either did not know the history of Bessarabia or, for the achievement of the communists's aim, considered that he could deny the fact that the Bessarabian Moldavians were part of the Romanian people and that their territory was part of the latter's national territory."[23]

It is necessary to add the following. Rubinstein belonged to an old family of Bessarabian Jews and thus, in my opinion, had every right to consider that Bessarabia was his *fatherland*. On the other hand, it is not at all unlikely that the investigator was from a different Romanian province and, in Rubinstein's view, this investigator was a "foreigner" on the land of Bessarabia. In Rubinstein's case, the land of Bessarabia was *possibly* the *fatherland* of a number of his predecessors' generations. But it was only the *adoptive fatherland* of these presumed generations, their *historical fatherland* being somewhere else. In the other case, however, that of the presumed investigator who came to Bessarabia after 1918, this province was *the historical fatherland* of his people, although he, as an individual, had been born and had lived on a different part of the territory of the Romanian people before 1918.

If the determining factor that guides us is the historical method, Transnistria and other territories east of Transnistria populated by Romanians must be considered *adoptive and not historical fatherlands* of the latter.

An important aspect of this problem is that during certain periods not only *adoptive fatherlands*, but also *historical* ones can be *hostile fatherlands*. The Transnistrian Romanians on the one hand, and the Bessarabian Gagauz and all the other non-Romanian nationalities that populate Bessarabia and Northern Bucovina on the other hand, are not *on the historical territory* of their respective peoples. Regarding the Romanians, this historical territory was marked by their ancestors who built fortresses on the right bank of

---

[23]Ibid.

the Dniester, and not elsewhere, on the banks of the Bug, for instance. And Mihai Eminescu's verses "De la Nistru pân' la Tisa/ Tot Românul plânsu-mi-s-a" ("From Tisa to Dniester's tide/ All Romanians to me cried") are not just a figure of speech (as someone tried to maintain in an issue of the weekly *Literatura și Arta*), but an artistic reflection of a concrete historical reality, namely the eastern and western borders of the national territory of the Romanians.

I realize perfectly well that this point of view may provoke the resentment of some Transnistrian Romanians (and not only Transnistrian) against me, and not only among the Romanians natives from the districts on the left side of the Dniester who today live on the Bessarabian territory of the Republic of Moldavia, but also of those who continue to live in the districts east of the Dniester, especially among those who have fought courageously to defend the national rights of the Romanians and their spiritual values. Thus, it is not surprising that the dichotomy *historical fatherland — adoptive fatherland* can be contested by many in the former Soviet Republic of Moldavia. First of all, because within its population there are considerable numbers of *Mankurts*, supported by those non-Romanian forces who attempt to re-establish, at any price, the former Soviet Empire.

What is surprising, however, regarding the publication of Nircă's diatribe, is the fact that the newspaper of the republic's government assumed in this case the role of messenger of the non-Romanian and *Mankurt* forces.

***

If we consider the consequences of the seizure of Bessarabia and Northern Bucovina, then *separatists* were such Bessarabian writers as Emilian Bucov, Andrei Lupan, David Vetrov, as well as Bessarabian communists who not only declared themselves for the annexation of the region, but supported it in various ways. They made common cause with the foreigners who *separated* Bessarabia (and Northern Bucovina along with the district of Herța) from the historical territory of the Romanian people.

If we refer to those in the south and the north of Bessarabia who did not take a position against the dismemberment of the province when, on 2 August 1940, the Union Republic was formed, but, on the contrary, supported Moscow's arbitrary actions, they were also *separatists*. In our days, Nircă, when using the term *integrated Moldavia* for the territory of the Republic of Moldavia, is in contradiction with the truth and, from a historical perspective, an inveterate *separatist*. E. Nircă was born and raised on the territory of the former *autonomous* republic on the left side of the Dniester. Naming the republic within its present borders *integrated Moldavia,* he approves not only of the dismemberment of Bessarabia, but also with the division of the territory of the *autonomous* republic by the law of 2 August 1940 and, from this point of view, he can be characterized as a *separatist*.

By the invective according to which I allegedly appealed to the publishing houses of Moldavia to publish my books, and "this call was heard" by the magazine *Basarabia*, Nircă actually criticized the magazine for publishing *Russia, Romania and Bessarabia*. Is it normal that the magazine has not reacted to Nircă's calumnies?

***

In one of his poems, the Bessarabian poet Grigore Vieru declared himself to be a *nationalist*, and, indeed, he is a nationalist, but a patriotic nationalist, and not a chauvinistic one. This great poet and great Romanian patriot wrote at the end of January 1993:

> "speaking of Transnistria, I would like to express my point of view regarding it, a strictly personal point of view which I do not want to impose on anyone. I myself am not so much alarmed that the imperial forces took Transnistria from us — I am afraid that they might give it back. Because by regaining Transnistria we would lose Bessarabia, more precisely we would diminish the chances for our reunification with Romania, if we will not lose them for good. It seems that the leadership of the Republic of Moldavia is aware of this, while the imperial Kremlin, which can not accept the loss of Bessarabia, knows it for certain. I do not want to be misunderstood: I do not reject the Romanians from Transnistria, but here is the truth: after

the unification, Tiraspol, specialized in diversions, would ask for autonomy within Romania, at the same time filling the country with spies."[24]

***

Regarding the dichotomy *historical fatherland — adoptive fatherland* we must add the following:

1. The event that took place in Bessarabia after the "Sfatul Țării" proclaimed it, on 2 (15) December 1917, the Democratic Moldavian Republic, and especially after the attempts by the Front Section (sent by Odessa) to take power failed, along with the latter's detachments many of those who were against the national self-determination of the native population of the region crossed over to the other side of the Dniester. Some of those who, at that time, left Bessarabia organized, in January 1918, in Tiraspol, a group of refugees which they named "The Revolutionary Committee for the Salvation of the Republic of Moldavia." The majority of those who created this committee were not Moldavians (the Voronov brothers, Bogdesco, Garber, Nikolsky, Dascal, Hatskilevich[25]), and the Republic of Moldavia which they intended "to save" did not include the territory on the left side of the Dniester. This is proven by the official bulletin published on 26 January 1918 by the newspaper *Golos revoliutsii* in Odessa, which said: "the committee intends to unite around it all the revolutionary elements in Bessarabia with the scope of fighting together to drive the Romanians away..."[26]

2. The terms *Moldavians* and *Moldavia* are not even mentioned in the resolution adopted by a group of refugees from the counties of Hotin, Bălți, and Soroca who met on 29-30 January (11-12 February) 1918 in the Ukrainian town Moghiliov-Podolsk and proclaimed themselves "The Central Executive Committee of the Soviets of the

---

[24]*Literatura și Arta*, 11 February 1993.

[25]A. Zvatur et al., *Letopis' vashneishikh sobytii istorii kommunisticheskoi partii Moldavii*. Kishinev, 1976, p. 86.

[26]N. Beresniakov et al., *Bor, ba trudiashchzkhsia Moldavii protiv interventov i vnutrennei kontrrevoliutsii. (1917-1920)*. Kishinev, 1967, p. 95.

Bessarabian Peasants', Workers', and Soldiers' Deputies."[27] It is clear that the Bessarabian refugees from Moghiliov-Podolsk (who, in their overwhelming majority, were not Moldavian either) were not influenced, like those from Tiraspol, by the fact that meanwhile Bessarabia had been proclaimed Democratic *Moldavian* Republic.

3. Referring to the period 1917-1918, A. Grecul, one of the most obedient Soviet historians, wrote: "Historians did not find sources that speak directly about the formation of a Soviet Moldavian or Bessarabian republic."[28] This confirms the above statements about the *Moldavian Republic* which the Bessarabian refugees from Tiraspol wanted "to save."

4. But, after the Democratic Moldavian Republic united with the historical fatherland of its native population and entered into the composition of the Romanian state under the name of Bessarabia, the Soviets, in their attempts to take over the territory between the Dniester and the Prut, also began to use this name which the Russian Empire had extended over the whole region seized in 1812. Thus, when, with a view to occupying the Romanian territories between the Dniester and the Prut, they staged, at the end of April and the beginning of May 1919, the creation of an alleged government in exile on the territory on the left side of the Dniester, they named it the Provisional Workers' and Peasants' Revolutionary Government of *Bessarabia*. In their overwhelming majority, the members of this so-called government were not Moldavian either (I. Krivorukov, Palamarenko, Aladjalov, G. Kasperovsky, M. Bujor, Z. Ushan[29]).

Based on a subjective interpretation of the historical events at best, or on their deliberate distortion at worst, those who maintain that the districts of the Republic of Moldavia on the left of the Dniester are historical lands of the Moldavian population mislead the public.

---

[27] Ibid., pp. 106-107.

[28] A. Grecul, *Rastsvet moldavskoi sotsialisticheskoi natsii*. Kishinev, 1974, p. 31.

[29] N. Berezniakov et al., op. cit., p. 295.

Dreptate — Promoters of Moscow's Imperial Interests

In December 1992 the bilingual newspaper *Dreptate* — *Spravedlivost'* began to appear in Chişinău, being edited by former members of the Communist Party (whose activity had been interdicted on the territory of the republic through a decision of the parliamentary presidium on 23 August 1991) who had changed their name to the Socialist Party of Moldavia. Already in the second issue of this publication Valerii Egorov, one of the members of the republican council of the so-called Socialist Party, declared openly: "The constitution and legislation of the Republic of Moldavia offers to our comrades in ideology the possibility to create, on the basis of the members and partisans of the former Communist Party, a party that does not renounce its ideas, but will be able to function in the new conditions and to carry out its initial mission — that of serving the interests of the working people."[30]

Indeed, in the Program Declaration of the Socialist Party of Moldavia, its new adherents repeat the slogans of their "old" party like, for instance: "We will contribute to the development of internationalist traditions, which were consolidated during the years of Soviet power, purifying them however of the scholastic slogans."[31] This purification proves to be, however, very selective, in the sense that, renouncing some of the "scholastic slogans" used not very long before by themselves, the former communists continue to obstinately use many others from their old terminology.

Thus, trained for years by the Communist Party "to say something and think something else" to disguise the truth about the policies they promoted in the Soviet Socialist Republic of Moldavia, the Socialists avoid in their newspaper such formulas that would be in contradiction with the "scholastic slogans" of their former party. For example, in the spirit of "internationalist traditions," the

---

[30]*Dreptate*, no. 2, December 1992.

[31]Ibid., no. 1, p. 4.

newspaper declares itself against "Moldavianophobia, Russianophobia, and Gagauzophobia."[32]

For decades, the Communist Party proclaimed its so-called internationalist policy and declared that the friendship amongst peoples, which crystallized under the influence of this policy, became an objective reality of the USSR in general and in all its national republics in particular. All these despite the fact that the Communist Party constantly promoted policies that are summarized by the famous formula "*divide et impera*" ("*divide and dominate*") with all its disastrous implications, from various points of view, for the non-Russian nationalities, including the native populations of the national republics.

The socialists, in the very first number of their newspaper, declare that they will contribute to "the development and enrichment of the experience accumulated regarding the friendship and solidarity among the nationalities of the republic," and that they will contribute "to the further development of the historical memory, of the national conscience and the dignity of the Moldavian people,... to the development of the internationalist traditions that were consolidated during the years of Soviet power..."[33]

But the enchanting language ("internationalism," "friendship among peoples," "development of the historical memory," etc.) constantly used by the Socialists is in flagrant contradiction with the real state of affairs in the republic. Their newspaper is filled with invectives, insults, and intimidations from the well-known terminology of the promoters of Moscow's policy in the non-Russian republics of the USSR. In this respect, it is enough to reproduce the following series of terms used in an article published in the first issue of the newspaper *Dreptate*: "incompetence, subjectivism, dilletantism, primitiveness, historical ignorance, preconceived ideas, dishonesty, falsifiers, renegades, etc."[34]

---

[32]Ibid., no. 1, p. 4.

[33]*Dreptate*, no. 1, December 1992, p. 4.

[34]Ibid., p. 6.

All these insults and invectives are used to defame and intimidate intellectuals who declare that they are Romanians, that their language is Romanian, and that Bessarabia, part of the historical territory of the Romanian people, was occupied by the Tsarist Empire in 1812 and by the Soviet Empire in 1940. A. Lazarev, who tries to denigrate those who are fighting for the unification of Bessarabia with Romania, says in one of his articles published in the same journal: "One resorts to deception and calumny when one lacks convincing arguments."[35]

As those from *Dreptate* consider, or rather want their readers to consider that they do not mislead, do not calumniate anyone, do not lack *convincing arguments* to substantiate their position, we will refer further on to the "arguments" presented as scientific by the authors of some articles published in this newspaper.

Since the appearance of the newspaper *Dreptate* in December 1992 until May 1993, Lazarev was present with his articles in almost every issue of the journal. We will refer now to one of his articles entitled "No Matter How Elevating the Aspiration Is, it Is Only an Idle Sound in the Face of Scientific Arguments."[36] In 1979, in my work *Rossia, Rumania i Bessarabia*, I insisted on some of the "scientific arguments" used by Lazarev in his writings. From the analysis of these arguments we drew conclusions resembling those of Constantin Giurescu. Those were Lazarev's arguments in his position as a Communist. Let us see now what are the "scientific arguments" of Lazarev the Socialist.

In an open letter addressed to the parliament of the republic, Lazarev uses violent communist terminology every time he refers to those members of parliament who consider that the natives of the Republic of Moldavia are Romanians, that their language is Romanian, and that sooner or later Bessarabia will unite with Romania. In this letter, the respective members of parliament are abused with insults like "unscrupulous," "enemies of everything that is Moldavian," etc.

---

[35]Ibid., no. 6 (8), April 1993, p. 6.

[36]A. Lazarev, "Zhelanie, dazhe smoe vosvyshennoe, iavliaetsia pustym zvukom protiv nauchnykh argumentov," in *Dreptate*, no. 1, no. 2, 1992, no. 1 (3) 1993.

The Minister of Culture, the talented actor and director Ion Ungureanu, is the recipient of another open letter written by Lazarev, in which the latter accuses him that he is guided by the preconceived ideas of incompetent people, that he joined the Popular Front of Moldavia, a certain group of those people who, out of *historical ignorance* and *theoretical incompetence*... assumed the unreal mission to "write the entire history of the Moldavian people,... rejecting everything that the historical sciences have achieved over the centuries."[37]

The framework of Lazarev's "scientific arguments" is centered around three fundamental terms that represent the Alpha and Omega of all his theories about the language, national identity, and the territory of the native population of the Republic of Moldavia. These terms are *glotonym* (name of a language), *ethnonym* (name of an ethnic group), and *toponym* (name of a place) and they appear in almost all the articles published by Lazarev and by other theoreticians of the Socialist Party in the newspaper *Dreptate*. And because these terms are used as principal arguments against the position of those who consider that they are Romanians, that their language is Romanian, and that Bessarabia was occupied by the Russians in 1940, we will refer further on to the objective reality reflected by these terms with regard to the language of the natives, their nationality, and the territory they populate.

Let us begin with the toponym Moldavia. In the open letter addressed to the parliament of the republic, Lazarev accuses more than once part of the deputies, and also "official members of the supreme legislative body of the Republic of Moldavia, the independent state of the Moldavian people," that "they do not recognize this people and its state as long as they are for the dissolution of the Moldavian people and the Republic of Moldavia and the transformation of the latter into a province of a different state." His principal argument in this respect is that the patriotic call of Stephen the Great was "Union, Moldavians," that "in his time no one talked or wrote about Romania, about Romanians, or about the Romanian language." We can contradict the historian Lazarev by

---

[37]*Dreptate*, no. 1, December 1992, p. 6.

saying that in Stephen the Great's times, as well as, let us say, during Alexandru Ioan Cuza's rule or later, no one ever talked nor wrote that the territory on which the present independent Republic of Moldavia lies had the geographical and political name of *Moldavia*. The toponym Moldavia used by Lazarev in his articles is, in fact, an invention of Moscow, which does not even cover the entire territory annexed by the Russians in 1812 from the Principality of Moldavia — Bessarabia — but only six of the nine counties of the Bessarabia of the year 1940 and a part of that organization which was created in 1924 under the name of the Autonomous Soviet Socialist Republic of Moldavia within the Soviet Ukraine.

"The achievements of the historical sciences," to which Lazarev refers, do not certify that the territory of the present Republic of Moldavia was ever called Moldavia. What the historical science attests to is that the territory of the six counties of Bessarabia, occupied by the Soviets in 1940, along with the territory of its other three counties, which in that same year Moscow gave to the Ukraine, were for many centuries part of the Principality of Moldavia, that between the years 1918 and 1940 the whole territory of Bessarabia was again part of the Romanian state after more than a century of foreign rule (1812-1918). This is the historical truth, just as it is true that the territory of the Autonomous Moldavian Republic created by Moscow in 1924 on the left side of the Dniester, despite the fact that it was populated also by Romanians (and continues to be), was never considered in "the achievements of the historical sciences" under the name of Moldavia. The Soviet imperialists demonstrated the artificiality of this toponym when they dissolved that republic in 1940.

Țara-de-Sus, Țara-de-Jos, Țara Moldovei, Țara Muntenească, Țara Românească, Țara Oltului, Țara Severinului, Țara Bârsei, Țara Crișului, Maramureș, Transylvania, the Banat, Oltenia, Muntenia, Moldavia, Dobrodgea, Bessarabia, and Bucovina are all historical subdivisions of the toponym Romania, as the names of Moldavians, Transylvanians, Bessarabians, and so on are all contextual (relative) synonyms for the Romanian nation, and thus constituent parts of the ethnonym Romanians. Using the ethnonym Moldavians as a "scientific argument" against his opponents who maintain that Moldavian is a contextual synonym of the ethnonym Romanian,

Lazarev expresses the preconceived ideas of the socialists from *Dreptate* who try to mislead the public opinion of the republic.

Alexei Mateevici's famous poem *Limba noastră* (*Our language*) has served to Lazarev and other *Mankurts* as an "indisputable" argument that *the Moldavian language* and not *the Romanian language* is the glotonym of the native population of the republic. But this argument breaks down immediately when we analyze not only its macro-context, but also its micro-context. Thus, when Alexei Mateevici says in his poem *Limba noastră*: "În rostirea ei bătrânii/ Cu sudori sfinţit-au ţara.../ ...Şi-ţi vedea cât e de darnic/ Graiul ţării noastre dragă" ("Speaking it our forefathers/ With their sweat hallowed our country.../ ...And you will see how very rich/ Is the tongue of our dear country") it is very clear that the word *ţară* — *country* (used twice by Mateevici in this great poem written in Chişinău on 17 June 1917) designates a totally different territorial meaning than the one proposed by Lazarev. And Alexei Mateevici's phrase "our language" designates *the Romanian language* and not *the Moldavian language*, the latter being considered by him, as well as by the overwhelming majority of the writers east and west of the Prut, as being a contextual synonym of the glotonym the Romanian language.

In an article published in two issues of the newspaper *Dreptate*, Vera Smelîh, who "more than sixty years ago was A. Lazarev's professor at the Moldavian Pedagogical Institute of Tiraspol," deals "with the Moldavians as a nation that has its own history, language, culture, and its own territory."[38] Stating that "the phrase *'the Romanian language'* began to be used more and more often instead of *'the Moldavian language'*" Vera Smelîh emphasizes that:"there is no doubt that the people of Moldavia have the right to the *glotonym* they have chosen and has been established as its own."[39]

Vera Smelov begins her article eulogizing A. Lazarev for his open letter addressed to Ion Ungureanu, the Minister of Culture, because "some representatives of the republic's intelligentsia, including official personalities, have a primitive and irresponsible

---

[38]*Dreptate*, no. 4 (6), March 1993, p. 6.

[39]Ibid.

attitude toward the historical sciences in general, toward concrete historical facts and events in Moldavia's history in general." After this preamble, she maintains that she has every reason to share "the position of Academician A. Lazarev" since in the course of a few decades she dealt with "the study of the history of Moldavia's philosophical and socio-political thinking," which obliged her to study and know "the history of the region and its prominent personalities."[40] She concentrates her attacks against the linguist Nicolae Mătcaş, the Minister of Science and Education, especially against his position regarding the problems of *the language*, and she does it with the same kind of "scientific" arguments as her former student.

Thus, declaring that "during the elaboration of the Law regarding the state language, serious mistakes were committed, caused by the irresponsible attitude of certain scientists toward facts of great importance for solving this problem,"[41] Smelîh accuses Mătcaş and Ion Demeniuc that they deliberately distorted the facts because "their political position" required it. As evidence, she reproduces the following fragment from an article published by the two linguists on 16 February 1989 in the newspaper *Vecernii Kishiniov*: "the classics of Moldavian and Romanian literature — Gheorghe Asachi, C. Stamati, A. Donici, Alecu Russo, Alexei Mateevici — fought for the Latin alphabet, wrote their work using it."

The "scientific" argument used by Smelîh against this statement is that Asachi and Stamati criticized "the Latinist school," that Mateevici showed that the Latinists began "to cleanse" the language of Slavic elements and introduce Latin elements. But not only the writers referred to by Smelîh criticized "the Latinist school." The overwhelming majority of the classics of Romanian literature rejected the exaggerations and the mistakes of the Latinists. But this does not mean that they were *against* the Latin alphabet. On the contrary: although they declared themselves against the Latinism promoted by

---

[40]Ibid.

[41]Ibid.

Samuil Micu, Gheroghe Șincai, and Petru Maior, they supported the change over to the Latin alphabet.

The use of a contextual synonym for the term *the Romanian language* cannot refute the truth confirmed by the most imposing Romanist scholars from all over the world, who in their Appeal of 2 April 1993 wrote very explicitly that "The language spoken in Moldavia east of the Prut is *the Romanian language*, a glotonym that should be made official, in conformity with the scientific and historical truth, in the constitution of the country (as well as the ethnonym *Romanians*, which does not mean that the inhabitants of Moldavia will cease to be, from a territorial point of view, Moldavians.)"[42]

This is the position expressed "in conformity with the scientific and historical truth" by the Romanist scholars who participated at the international colloquium "Romania: Typology, Classification, Characteristics," organized by the Institute of Romance Philology of the University of Munich and by Sudoesteuropa-Gesellschaft between 30 March and 2 April 1993. And as much as Lazarev, Senic, and others will try to threaten and intimidate their opponents, they will not be able to impose their "theories" again, except in the case of a total transformation of the republic into a colony of the Russian Empire, as it was under the Soviet rule.

The appearance at the end of 1992 of the first issue of the newspaper *Dreptate* reflected a change that took place in the political situation in the Republic of Moldavia. That change finally led to the resignation of Alexandru Moșanu as president of the parliament, of the poet Ion Hadârcă as first vice-president of the parliament, and of Valeriu Matei and V. Nedelciuc as members of the presidium of the parliament. The new political situation encouraged the communist forces, in their new posture as Socialists, to raise their heads. All the articles published in *Dreptate*, dealing in one way or another with the fundamental problem for the fate of the native population — unification with Romania or affiliation with the CIS — show that the Socialists are the continuers of the Communists's "cause" and promote, in fact, Moscow's interests in the Republic of Moldavia.

---

[42]"Apel," *Literatura și Arta*, 22 April 1993.

II. MANNA FOR THE MANKURTS

Soviet Realities in the Distorted View of Certain Western Researchers

In 1981 Irina Livezeanu published an article entitled "Urbanization in a Low Key and Linguistic Change in Soviet Moldavia" in two issues of the magazine *Soviet Studies* in Glasgow. This article determined me to prepare a material about the real state of affairs in Moldavia east of the Prut River, because, as I wrote to the editor of the magazine on 22 May 1982, Irina Livezeanu's article "made me write my article because not only the general conclusions of the author, but also certain data reproduced in her article are not in accordance with the realities in Soviet Moldavia." We underlined deficiencies in Irina Livezeanu's article such as her assertions that:

a) *before 1812... the bulk of the territory, today included in the SSR of Moldavia*, formed the eastern part of the Principality of Moldavia and *was known under the geographic name of Bessarabia*.[43] (But before 1812 Bessarabia was *a historical and not a geographic name*, and the bulk of the territory known then under this name, in other words the south of the region, which was annexed in 1812 by the Russian Empire, was not included in 1940 in the SSR of Moldavia, but in the SSR of the Ukraine);

---

[43] *Soviet Studies*, vol. XXXIII, no. 3, 1981, p. 328.

b) in 1940, the SSR of Moldavia was formed of *the largest part of the occupied territory*, the largest part of *the three southern counties* being included in the SSR of the Ukraine.[44] (But in 1940 the largest part not of three, but *of two southern counties* (Cetatea Albă and Ismail) plus a northern county (Hotin) were included in the SSR of the Ukraine);

c) in 1944 Bessarabia "reverted" under Soviet rule, being again called Moldavia.[45] (But in 1944, as after the events of the year 1940, only part of Bessarabia was included in the SSR of Moldavia).

But the main objection I made to Irina Livezeanu's article is that, announcing in the title that the article will deal not only with urbanization, but also with "linguistic changes," she maintains in her article, in flagrant contradiction with the objective situation in the SSR of Moldavia in the period under examination, that during that time there was no concerted policy of encouraging the spread of the Russian language and culture to the detriment of the national language of the natives[46] and that the Soviet Government helped the perpetuity of the linguistic diversity in the republic.[47]

The formulations to which Livezeanu sometimes resorts — "in January 1918, after the Russian revolution, Bessarabia became, for a short time, an independent republic, after which *it was integrated* into Romania after 1940;" "after the Hitler-Stalin pact, the Soviet troops *occupied* Bessarabia;" "in 1941 the whole Bessarabia *was recaptured* by Romanian troops;" "in 1944 *Bessarabia reverted* to Soviet rule"[48] — denote the lack of a well-defined position in the evaluation of the *essence* of the historical events, or the avoidance of an objective and principled treatment of the latter. The dodging becomes even more evident when we read footnote 17 of the first part of her article, which reads as follows: "as it is not our purpose to solve the problem whether the native inhabitants of Bessarabia or the

---

[44]Ibid., p. 329.

[45]Ibid.

[46]Ibid., no. 4, 1981, p. 582.

[47]Ibid., p. 584.

[48]Ibid., no. 3, p. 328-329.

SSR of Moldavia are, by their ethnic origin, Romanians or Moldavians, for each period taken into consideration we accepted the terminology used by the respective governing power to denote the nationality and the language of the native population."[49]

We should also mention here that the sources used by Livezeanu were, on the one hand, the Soviet censuses, and, on the other hand, theses and formulations elaborated by obedient Soviet authors, as Iu. Arutunyan, R. Tadevosyan, N. Guboglo, V. Zeleniuc, etc. But, even certain Soviet specialists, both before and after Gorbachev's reorganization, as well as especially during the last years, repeatedly wrote in their works that the data of the Soviet censuses are lacking,[50] and in the non-Russian republics, the Soviet "scholars," whose writings served as sources for Livezeanu, are called, with good reason, *Mankurts* who promote Moscow's national policy.

In 1986 Livezeanu published a review of my book *Naţiuni, poporaţii, popor. Studiu asupra politicii naţionale a partidului comunist în Moldova Sovietică* (1984) in which, in the usual... Soviet style, she denigrates not only the study, which according to her presents unacceptable opinions, but also the author himself. Thus, in the respective journal,[51] Livezeanu maintains that the first of the three assertions in my book suffers "from intellectual carelessness," that "this lack of logical reasoning is evident in Bruchis's attempt to demonstrate" that "in his obsession with Moscow's unrelenting manipulation,... Bruchis ignores open-ended historical processes," that "the statistics cited do not by themselves suggest any concerted policy."

We could mention here other such "appreciations," but by the one quoted above Livezeanu proves that she persists in maintaining the principal thesis of her article published in 1981, namely that in Soviet Moldavia the authorities did not promote a concerted policy during the respective period.

---

[49]Ibid., p. 348.

[50]V. Kozlov, *Natsional 'nosti S.S.S.R. Etnograficheskii obzor*, 2nd ed., Moscow, 1982.

[51]*Slavic Review*, vol. 44, no. 4, 1986, pp. 741-742.

Many Western scholars specialized in the problems of the USSR deserve to be respected as well-intentioned people who, in their research, present Soviet realities the way they are, in all their complexity, and the way they should be treated and interpreted after an unbiased analysis of their real substance. However, there are, at the same time, other Western researchers who allow themselves to be misled by the data provided by statistics made up by the promoters of Moscow's national policy and by theses and formulas elaborated on the basis of these statistics. Livezeanu belongs, at best, to this last group of Western researchers. We say at best because she pretends to be a friend of the Romanian people. It is not surprising that the inveterate *Mankurt* F. Angheli eulogizes the article published by Livezeanu in 1981 and places its author among those Western scholars who "appreciate objectively the experience of the USSR in solving the national problem and the language problem."[52]

***

It is abhorrent to maintain, as results from Irina Livezeanu's article, that only after the re-annexation of Bessarabia in 1940 (and afterwards in 1944) by the Soviets, in other words that only under P. Borodin, L. Salagor, D. Gladchi, Z. Serdiuk, N. Coval, L. Brezhnev, I. Bodiul, that is only under the "satraps" who promoted the Kremlin's policy of Russification and denationalization of the native population, the level of cultural orientation of the Moldavian population changed (for the better)! In 1989 Dennis Deletant appreciated Irina Livezeanu's work as being "a valuable study on urbanization and linguistic change in the republic; an equilibrium between Moldavian and Russian seems to have been established."[53] Deletant continues, in flagrant contradiction with the facts revealed by prominent scientists and scholars from the Republic of Moldavia,

---

[52]F. Angheli, "Narody S.S.S.R. za dvuiazychie: pricem tut russifikatsia?" in *Sovetskaia Moldavia*, 23 July 1986.

[53]D. Deletant, "Language Policy and Linguistic Trends in Soviet Moldavia," in M. Kirkwood, ed., *Language Planing in the Soviet Union*, Basingstoke and London, 1989, p. 199.

saying that "the data analyzed above does not warrant alarm about the extent to which the Moldavian population has been linguistically Russified."[54]

In 1991, Michael Kirkwood, the editor of Deletant's article, wrote in *Soviet Studies* that "the growing importance of Russian did not at once lead to a diminution in the importance of other Soviet languages."[55]

Critics of the Book *One Step Back, Two Steps Forward*[56]

Just affirmations and conclusions regarding the realities generated by the Soviet regime in the Republic of Moldavia are sometimes distorted even in works that appeared in the West, whose authors usually do not know either the language or the history of the Romanians east of the Prut. For example, the work *One Step Back, Two Steps Forward* was severely criticized on the one hand for its numerous typographical errors, attributed by the reviewer G. Shevelov[57] to the incompetence of its author, and, on the other hand, mainly because we did not deal in the respective work "with the differences between the Moldavian language and the Romanian language."[58] However, what we underline very explicitly in the work reviewed by the American professor Shevelov is that:

a) at the beginning of the 1950s a process of identification of the *literary* language of the Romanians east of the Prut with the Romanian language began;

---

[54]Ibid., p. 212.

[55]Michael Kirkwood, "Glasnost', 'The National Question,' and Soviet Language Policy," in *Soviet Studies*, vol. 45, no. 1, 1991, p. 63.

[56]Michael Bruchis, *One Step Back, Two Steps Forward. On the Language Policy of the Communist Party of the Soviet Union in the National Republics. (Moldavia: A Look Back, a Survey, and Perspectives, 1924-1980)*. Boulder-New York, 1982.

[57]*Canadian Slavonic Papers*, vol. XXV, no. 2, 1983, pp. 321-322.

[58]Ibid., p. 322

b) the *spoken* language of these Romanians, as a consequence of the national policy promoted by Moscow, was increasingly transformed into a Moldavian-Russian jargon;

c) the Russian language is extending more and more its social functions in the republic, to the detriment of the natives's language;

d) this is a general phenomenon in the USSR, and it is only a matter of the more or less rapid pace at which it manifests itself in one republic or another.

Regarding the negligence with which the correction of the manuscript was made, we wrote to the editor on 5 October 1982: "I am very sorry that you did not have the proofs sent to me so that I could personally make the corrections. I involuntarily offered some eventual critics from the USSR the possibility to use the deficiencies in the correction to denigrate the book and its author. I hope that any well-intentioned reader will realize that it is a matter of deficiencies that do not change either the essence of the book, or the facts presented in it."

It turned out, however, that such critics appeared not only in the USSR. What is relevant is the fact that in Western scholarly journals that I read, the number of those who criticized the book (2) is incomparably smaller than the number of those who praised it (9). Besides, the first two do not know the Romanian language, while six of those who wrote positive reviews know Romanian very well. It is no less significant that the majority of the reviewers who praised the book underlined at the same time the fact that it is filled with typographic mistakes.

We cannot say that Ch.R. Foster, the second Western reviewer who did not favorably review the book *One Step Back...*, tried deliberately to denigrate the book and its author, as G. Shevelov did. But Foster's negative appreciations are at least disputable, if not inconsistent. For example, Foster writes: Bruchis considers Moldavia, which includes Bessarabia taken away from Romania in 1940, as a homogenous unity from a linguistic viewpoint. This supposition allows him to treat as irrelevant any difference from the norm existent in Romania."[59]

---

[59]*Canadian Review of Studies in Nationalism*, vol. XI, no. 1, 1984, p. 166.

But V. Stati did not take into consideration the criteria on which the above-mentioned Western authors based their observations, namely preconceived ideas, having no connection with the object of their criticism.

Even the critical observations from the positive reviews proved to be "manna" for Stati. Thus, the majority of the Western authors of such reviews mentioned both the negligent correction of the work *One Step Back...*, as well as its often inadequate translation. And they were perfectly right. But even in those cases when a critical observation (regarding the form and not the essence of the work) from such a review is not totally justified, it is used by others as proof for our "ignorance and incompetence." Thus, Dennis Deletant wrote that in "*One Step Back...* the reader encounters a whole series of acronyms of the name *Soviet Moldavia*," and goes on by saying: "thus we find that *AR* (*Autonomous Republic*) (p. 66), *MAR* (*Moldavian Autonomous Republic*) (p. 62) and *Moldavian ASSR* (p. 49) are all used do designate *the Autonomous Moldavian Soviet Socialist Republic* which was created on 1 October 1924 on the left bank of the Dniester River. In the title of chapter 3 the author further confuses the reader by using the term *Union Moldavian Republic of the Soviet Union* to designate *the Moldavian Soviet Socialist Republic* which was created on 2 August 1940."[60]

I have to say that this long fragment surprised me when I first read the review, and this is why:

a) Deletant knew very well that the reviewed text was a translation (and, besides, a deficient translation). However he maintained that "the author further confuses the reader."

b) Acronyms are widely used in British scientific texts. For example, the term *The United States of America* is usually abbreviated as USA or US.

c) In historiography, linguistics, and the history of literature of Moldavia east of the Prut, the formulations *autonomous republic* and *union republic* are widely circulated terms. Thus, the reviewer did not have any reason to accuse the author that he "confuses the reader."

---

[60]*The Slavonic and East European Review*, vol. 62, no. 1, 1984, p. 106.

In order to prove our incompetence and, besides, that we "serve those who pay more," Stati distorts the texts reproduced in the work *One Step Back...*, and amputates certain quotations from foreign sources or from translations in such a way that he perverts the real sense of the affirmation that he is commenting on.

For example, the fragment we quoted from Deletant's review, together with Stati's comments, appears in "Limba românească şi rǎuvoitorii ei" ("The Moldavian language and its enemies") in the following translation, here and there amputated, here and there distorted:

> "Bruchis's ambition to make 'discoveries' at any price, to put into circulation formulations which are both tendentious as well as ridiculous, bothered the British reviewer as well. Dennis Deletant writes, disconcerted, that 'the reader permanently encounters anachronisms. Thus, we find that AR — the Autonomous Republic, MAR — Moldavian Autonomous Republic are synonyms of the Moldavian ASSR. In the title of the third chapter the author shocks his reader even more by using the term Union Moldavian Republic of the Soviet Union to designate the Moldavian Soviet Socialist Republic.'"[61]

Had Stati consulted the dictionary, he would have discovered that the word *acronym* means *abbreviation*, and not *anachronism*.

In *Cultura şi lupta ideologică* Stati maintains that "the scope" of bourgeois propagandists "is to undermine the cohesion and friendship among Soviet peoples," and to exemplify this affirmation he adds: "The same Bruchis writes in black and white: 'For the appearance in Soviet conditions of the possibilities for the revival of the languages about to disappear and for their transformation into languages with complete value there is the need of... a qualitative leap that would fundamentally change the Soviet regime.' Neither more or less! Either the fundamental 'leap' will take place, or the 'specialist' continues, 'without such a leap, absolutely all the non-Russian

---

[61]Ibid., p. 106.

languages within the USSR are threatened with an inherent total disappearance."[62] However, in *One Step Back...* we maintained the following: "For the appearance in the Soviet regime of the possibility for the revival of the perverted languages of the non-Russian peoples within the USSR, and for the transformation of these languages into multilaterally developed languages, there is the need, as in the times when the Tsarist autocracy was overthrown, for a qualitative leap from a historical point of view to fundamentally change the Soviet regime. Without such a leap absolutely all the non-Russian languages within the USSR are facing an *inevitable* total disappearance."[63]

These were the last words of the book *One Step Back, Two Steps Forward*. And at the end of the first chapter, entitled "The Social Functions of the Russian Language," we wrote the following: "Under the influence of the Russian language, structural changes take place to a certain extent in all the non-Russian languages. Not only does the Russian language evict the non-Russian languages more and more from their most important social functions, but it also destroys them from within, paving the way for their gradual disappearance. Considering a series of objective and subjective causes, the rate and forms of removing the non-Russian languages are different. However, despite the fact that in one or another national state of the Soviet peoples the rate and form of the respective language's removal can differ from the rate and form of another languages's removal, the general tendency in absolutely all the republics, regions, and national districts is identical. This tendency can be noticed in the state activity, in the party activity, in schools, in scientific, pedagogical, and cultural life, in which the preponderance of the Russian language is overwhelming."[64]

The philologists V. Bahnaru and C. Tănase wrote an article demonstrating that a) the social functions of the (non-Russian languages) were reduced to the minimum, that b) "the language (of the Romanians from the Republic of Moldavia) is excluded from

---

[62]V. Stati, *Cultura și lupta ideologică. Împotriva falsificatorilor culturii Moldovei Sovietice*. Chișinău, 1987, p. 67.

[63]Michael Bruchis, op. cit., p. 314.

[64]Ibid., p. 22.

administration, science, etc.," that c) "the disastrous situation of the language" is a direct consequence of the fact that, on the one hand, "more than a century of Tsarist domination led to the total degradation of the Moldavian language," and, on the other hand, "that the serious distortions of the Leninist national policy reduced almost completely the social functions of the Moldavian language."[65]

All these facts (with the exception, of course, of "the Leninist national policy," which was allegedly distorted) were examined in *One Step Back. Two Steps Forward*. However, Stati characterized this work as "anti-Moldavian" and me as a renegade, as "one of the civil servants paid by imperialist propaganda."[66]

---

[65] *Orizontul*, no. 2, 1989, pp. 29, 32.

[66] V. Stati, *Limba moldovenească...*, pp. 122-123.

CONCLUSION

The elections of 27 February 1994 ended with the clear victory of those forces that did everything to disunite and defame the patriots who animated the large masses of the native population in the fight for the spiritual values of their people. The intimidation campaign of those who had brought President Snegur to power was taking ever more dreadful forms as the latter was yielding to Moscow's neo-imperialist pressures and drawing nearer to those forces that were fiercely fighting even the possibility of a development of the events that could lead to a new unification of the Romanian people. On 5 February 1994, a few weeks before the parliamentary elections, a large assembly, named by its organizers the Congress "Casa noastră — Republica Moldova" ("Our Home — The Republic of Moldavia"), gathered in the National Palace of Chişinău. The speech delivered by Snegur at this meeting, which the patriotic poet Nicolae Dabija described as the 16th Congress of the Communist Party of the SSR of Moldavia,[1] demonstrated once again that Mircea Snegur was on the side of Lazarev, Senic, Stati, and all the others like them.

---

[1] Nicolae Dabija, "Un congres al ruşinii," in *Literatura şi Arta*, 10 February 1994.

Not only this programmatic speech by the president, but also the speeches by the participants who took the floor, as well as the reaction of the audience at their words are very relevant. On 5 February the forces that a few weeks later won the overwhelming majority of mandates in the parliament of the republic, gathered, on the one hand, a docile and servile meeting in favor of the policy that was then promoted by the authorities, and, on the other hand, a provocative and aggressive assembly regarding the attitude toward those who considered unification with Romania as the salvation of the ethnic national being of the native population.

The speech made by the president of the republic on 5 February is full of theses and formulas that are not only ambiguous, but also in flagrant disagreement with the truth. This is why, in an open letter addressed to President Snegur and published on 24 February, a group of historians declared, among other things: "What you are trying to prove to the population of the republic... is that the Romanians on the other side of the Prut are not Romanians, but Moldavians..., your 'Moldavianism,' besides being anti-scientific, anti-national, and anti-historical, is essentially Romanianophobic."[2]

Revolted at the form, and especially the contents of the president's speech, the historians also wrote: "you ask us openly to falsify the chronicles, to distort the written work of our great predecessors... you even show us how to do it."[3]

Further on, the historians refer, among other things, to the work *Moldovenii în istorie*, which appeared especially for the Congress of 5 February, saying that "this revolting book, allegedly a historical work, is nothing but an attempt at the argumentation of the 'historical ideas' in your speech (of the president's speech)."

On 5 March, five of the most servile Soviet authors tried to contest, in an article published in the newspaper of the Agrarian Party, the open letter (of the 49 historians who signed it) and to substantiate the position of President Snegur as it had been presented a month before, at the congress "Our Home — The Republic of

---

[2] "Pericolul aservirii politice a veşnicelor adevăruri. Scrisoare deschisă domnului Mircea Snegur," în *Literatura şi Arta*, 24 February 1994.

[3] Ibid.

Moldavia." But their article proved once again that they did not renounce their way of not reflecting in their writings the national interests of the natives, but the policy promoted by the forces that served the imperial interests of Moscow.

Considering the arguments of the four signatories (P. Bîrnea, C. Stratievschi, V. Ţaranov, and V. Stati) of the "riposte" addressed to those 49 historians, as well as the way in which they contest the latter, we can presume that all four of them contributed in one way or another to the elaboration of the speech delivered by Mircea Snegur on 5 February 1994. Despite their metamorphoses, Stati, Lucinschi, Senic, and all those from their camp remained devout communists. After 27 February 1994, when they succeeded in obtaining the overwhelming majority of mandates in the parliament, Lucinschi, who not long before had popularized "dialogue, consensus, and compromise," revealed his true image. On 26 March the newspaper *Pămînt şi Oameni* of the Agrarian Party published a declaration entitled "Din apărare în ofensivă"[4] ("From Defence to Offensive") (in the Russian version of Lucinschi's newspaper the title is more aggressive — "Ot oborony k shirokomu nastupleniu,"[5] which in an accurate translation means, according to the real meaning of the adjective *shirokii* in this context, offensive *on the whole front*). The double dealing policy of the leaders of the Agrarian Party is reflected also by other differences that appear when we compare the two versions of the declaration. Thus, in the version addressed to the native population, Romanianophobia is somehow concealed in comparison with the one openly displayed in the version addressed to the Russians and the Russophones.

When we read in the declaration of the so-called pro-Moldavia patriots about the option of the Moldavian people "for an authentic democracy and for national dignity, for the unconditional independence of the Moldavian state," or about "the policy... of the Union forces" which were allegedly aiming at "undermining the Moldavian statehood, at cultivating among the young generation the lack of

---

[4] *Pămînt şi Oameni*, 26 March 1994.

[5] *Zemlia i Liudi*, 26 March 1994.

historical memory and values foreign to the Moldavians,"[6] it is not difficult to realize that those who elaborated the declaration of the so-called patriotic movement and those who published it are trying to revive outspokenly the Soviet methods of silencing the masses under their domination and of misleading international public opinion by using words and phrases with a diametrically opposed meaning to the one they have in the common language for defining those objective realities to which they refer.

Their advice that "the President, the reelected parliament, and the Government of Moldavia should pass from an indecisive defence to ample offensive actions, to the purge of historical falsehood and aggressive ideological Unionism, cultivated during the last three or four years,"[7] shows very clearly that in the Republic of Moldavia the ideological repertory of the communists who always used to blame others for their actions is again placed in action.

Those who now govern criticize the disastrous effects of the policy promoted in the Republic of Moldavia by Moscow and by their predecessors who served its interests. Thus, on 27 August 1992, Mircea Snegur declared the following:

> "The policy of excessive specialization, which was supposed to transform Moldavia into a 'blooming garden' of the Union, led to the artificial division of our potential into the super-agrarian 'right bank' and the super-industrial 'left bank,' to a super-integration in the economic space of the former USSR and in the area of the dying ruble."[8]

In the same manner, when Moscow unexpectedly brought him from Tadjikistan and named him first secretary of the Communist Party of the Republic of Moldavia, Lucinschi talked, in the report presented at the 17th Congress of the Moldavian Communist Party,

---

[6] Ibid.

[7] Ibid.

[8] *Nezavisimaia Moldavia*, 28 August 1992.

about the "long decades of distortions, falsification, and dissimulation," about "the aspirations and tendencies of the Moldavian people toward its national revival," emphasizing at the same time that "under the pretext of internationalization, the traditions and customs of the people were vanishing in the dark, any allusions to the common ethnic roots, culture, and language of the Moldavians and the Romanians were being obstructed."[9]

The present president of the parliament and leader of the Agrarian Party, Petru Lucinschi, worried by the consequences of the failed putsch of 19-21 August 1991, declared in an interview:

> "I do not intend to be a member of political organizations, to join any political structures. I am being offered various positions, I will think them over and decide what I will do. I need time. I think it best that new people should come and demonstrate their capacities... If we (in the context: the communists) hold on to power, we will not escape this circle. We will be accused again of all the failures."[10]

However, after a short time, not only did Lucinschi join political organizations and structures, but he did his best to bring in his former subordinates (V. Cherdivarenco, D. Nidelcu, I. Guţu, V. Iovv, Vasile Stati, and others). The fact that Vasile Stati is still among the "comrades of ideas" of the president of the parliament shows that they will try to revive in one way or another the old slogans of the imperialist policy regarding the language and history of the native population of the Republic of Moldavia.

No less "spectacular" were Mircea Snegur's change of positions during the last years. Lucinschi used during these years, as in the past, the term *republic* as a synonym for Soviet Moldavia and, respectively, the Republic of Moldavia, and the terms *country* and *Union,* as synonyms for the USSR. However, Mircea Snegur

---

[9]*Sovetskaia Moldavia*, 18 May 1990.

[10]Petru Lucinschi, "N-am de gând să mă mai ocup de politică," *Nezavisimaia Moldova*, 5 December 1991.

(especially after the parliament adopted the "Declaration of Independence of the Republic of Moldavia on 27 August 1991"[11]) constantly used the term *country* only as a synonym for the terms *Republic* and *Republic of Moldavia*, and not for the term *USSR*. And even after he signed, on 21 December 1991 in Alma-Ata, along with eleven other presidents of former Soviet republics, the Declaration of the Constitution of the Community of Independent States (CIS), Mircea Snegur continued to use the term *country* only as an absolute synonym for the terms *Republic* and *Republic of Moldavia*.

Carried away by the enthusiasm of the native population and animated by the patriotic intelligentsia, Mircea Snegur contributed to the adoption of the law regarding the state language and the Latin alphabet (31 August 1989), as well as of the law regarding the National Flag (27 April 1990). Under the influence of the same enthusiasm, Mircea Snegur played an important role both in the adoption of the Declaration of Sovereignty of the SSR of Moldavia (23 June 1990), as well as in the adoption of the Declaration of Independence of the Republic of Moldavia (27 August 1991). But only three months after the adoption of the Declaration of Independence, Mircea Snegur went to Alma-Ata to sign the famous Declaration of the Constitution of the CIS. The signing by Snegur of the republic's adherence to the CIS was not, however, fortuitous. President Snegur had long before begun to deviate from the principles of those who had brought him to power and supported him to maintain his position when Lucinschi competed with him for the position of president of the Supreme Soviet of the republic. The plots, intrigues, and pressures associated with Moscow's neo-imperialism, and the intimidation and disconcerting of the masses of the native population by the internationalist *Mankurts* and Russophones of the "Edinstvo" movement and by other forces hostile to the national aspirations of the Romanians east of the Prut, as well as divisions within the popular front, due to a great extent to the fact that the president of the republic was increasingly supporting the *Mankurts* and, in general, the former communist nomenclature, all contributed Mircea Snegur's radical change of position.

---

[11] V. Nedelciuc, *Republica Moldova*, Chişinău, 1992, p. 13.

CONCLUSION

Thus, Snegur declared in a report presented on 2 September 1990 that "the intolerance of the separatists (in the context: of the Gagauz) would not have gone so far had it not been encouraged and directed by Moscow's anti-structuralist forces," and that "a battalion from the Ministry of Internal Affairs of the USSR, stationed in Chişinău, was sent to Tiraspol to secure the development of the proceedings of the so-called congress of deputies of all levels from the Nistrian localities," after which he concluded: "let us see who will try now to maintain that Moscow does not direct the actions of destabilization within the republic."[12]

However, a year and some months later, on 24 December 1991, after the signing of the Alma-Ata Declaration, a totally different Snegur came before the parliament, threatening those who were against the adhering to the CIS, declaring that "those who are against the policy have no moral right and especially no juridical right to occupy leading positions in a state whose existence they doubt."[13]

The distortions which abound in the speech delivered by Mircea Snegur at the congress "Our Home — The Republic of Moldavia" (a regional cliché of the slogan "Our Home — The Soviet Union" used during the Gorbachev period) are based on the attempts of A. Lazarev, V. Senic, Vasile Stati, and the others from their camp to revive in one way or another the slogans and theories elaborated under the Soviet regime.

Anyone who is familiar with the policy promoted in Bessarabia by the Tsarist invaders (during 1812-1917) and by the Soviet ones (1940-1941 and from 1944 on), as well as with the consequences of this policy, can see that the president of the Republic of Moldavia became a spokesman for the Russophones and the *Mankurts*, inspired, instigated, supported, and guided by Moscow.

---

[12] Mircea Snegur, "Să ne apărăm demnitatea de neam," *Literatura şi Arta*, 6 September 1990.

[13] Mircea Snegur, "Sud'ba naroda zavisit ot nashego politicheskogo myshlenia," in *Nezavisimaia Moldova*, 26 December 1991.

00198 0872